singing mother home

"DIXIE GIRL"

Lyrics By
Donna Davenport

Copyright 1999
By
Donna Davenport

Music By
Edward Corre

O DIX- IE GIRL THE MORN- ING'S COOL; THE BREEZE IS SOFT, THERE'S SUN- SHINE ON YOUR FACE. O DIX- IE GIRL, YOU CAN CLOSE YOUR EYES AND DRIFT THROUGH TIME ON DAYS TOUCHED BY LOVE AND GRACE. "COME HOME, COME HOME MY LIT- TLE DIX- IE GIRL, IT'S TIME AND TIME TO COME O HOME; COME FLY WITH US AS WE GO ON MY LIT- TLE GIRL, MY PRE- CIOUS ONE. O DIX- IE GIRL, JUST RE- MEM- BER HOW FREE YO RAN WITH DARK HAIR FLY- ING LOOSE; NOW, DIX- IE GIRL YOU CAN FLY A- GAIN, LET GO AND SOAR, TOUCH

DIXIE GIRL

EARTH AND HEA- VEN TOO 'COME HOME, COME HOME MY

LIT- TLE DIX- IE GIRL; IT'S TIME AND TIME TO COME ON

HOME; COME FLY WITH US AS WE GO ON,

MY LIT- TLE GIRL, - MY PRE- CIOUS ONE

JUST LOOK WHO'S HERE TO TAKE YOU HOME; AND, DIX- IE

GIRL, SEE ALL THE JOY YOU BRING! YOUR FA- THER SANG 'GOOD

BYE, GOOD- BYE" TO YOU AND NOW A- GAIN YOUR

FA- THER'S HERE TO SING: "COME HOME, COME HOME MY

LIT- TLE DIX- IE GIRL, IT'S TIME AND TIME TO COME ON

HOME; COME FLY WITH US AS WE GO ON

MY LIT- TLE GIRL, MY PRE- CIOUS ONE"

Singing Mother Home

A Psychologist's Journey through Anticipatory Grief

Donna S. Davenport

University of North Texas Press
Denton, Texas

Permissions:
University of North Texas Press
P.O. Box 311336
Denton, TX 76203-1336

The paper used in this book meets the minimum requirements of the
American National Standard for Permanence of Paper for Printed Library
Materials, z39.48.1984. Binding materials have been chosen for durability.

Library of Congress Cataloging-in-Publication Data
Davenport, Donna S.
 Singing mother home : a psychologist's journey through anticipatory
grief / Donna S. Davenport.
   p. cm.
Includes bibliographical references (p.   ).
 ISBN 1-57441-162-4
 1. Grief. 2. Bereavement--Psychological aspects. 3. Loss
(Psychology) 4. Mothers--Death--Psychological aspects. 5. Mothers
and daughters. I. Title.
 BF575.G7 D365 2003
 155.9'37--dc21
                              2002152765

Design by Angela Schmitt

Dedication

To the memory of Dixie
And to Bubba and Dixie Lee, family teammates

La hora es transparente:
vemos, si es invisible el pajaro,
el color de su canto.

> *The time is transparent:*
> *even if the bird is invisible*
> *let us see the color of his song.*

—Octavio Paz, translated by Muriel Rukeyser

Contents

Foreword

For most of the twenty-five years that I have known Donna Davenport, I've dreaded the day her mother died, for one couldn't know Donna without realizing how important Dixie was in her daughter's life. During these twenty-five years, Donna has been busy providing psychotherapy, teaching psychology at the doctoral level, and writing professional books and articles. More to the point, she possesses a finely honed intelligence, a dry wit, and a deep sense of compassion and understanding that she brings to bear upon those who know her. When I finally met Dixie, I began to see where it all began.

Dixie Davenport was a small and elegant lady. Her pride was mostly expressed in a firm, well-formed character, for she was indeed a person who quietly lived the values she espoused. Her pride was also evident in her dress. A few years ago, Donna and I took my elderly (and also elegant) Aunt Elizabeth and Dixie to the lake in northern New Jersey where Elizabeth grew up and I spent all my childhood vacations. It was a blazingly beautiful fall and the last two weeks the lake was open to visitors: a cool, quiet time with most of the summer folk gone. We had fires at night and spent the days walking in the woods, canoeing, and generally tramping around. Elizabeth kept taking me aside and making sotto voce comments about how beautiful Dixie looked and how well she was dressed. Everything matched. Everything was bright and beautiful. Dixie, with her petite, perfectly postured body and white, bobbed hair always looked like she had just stepped off a fashion runway. In my entire life, I'd never known my aunt to express the slightest insecurity about her appearance. But she did around Dixie.

Shortly after Dixie's death, Donna spent the weekend at my house. Exhausted from the demands of shuttling back and forth between Dixie's bedside in Dallas and maintaining a regular teaching and counseling schedule in Bryan, Donna slept most of the time. Finally she went out to her car and brought in boxes of lace and crochet and handsewn clothes to show me—things her great-grandmothers, grandmother, great-aunts, and mother made for themselves and their children. We sat on the floor and spilled out a hundred and fifty years of tiny baby garments covered with delicate embroidery, dresses for growing girls, crocheted collars, and nightgowns and petticoats for the women. One of these pieces epitomizes Dixie to me: a handmade pale lemon yellow organdy shift from her college days, as light as a ray of sun. Sandwiched between the two layers of organdy on the front, fabric prints of pink roses were glimpsed dimly through the organdy—as elegant a touch as any dress I've ever seen. It was understated, quiet, vibrant, and as lovely as she was.

I don't think I've ever known another person who loved her mother as much as Donna. As a therapist, it is common for me to see the malformations of great love into symbiosis or twists of love and hate. But Donna and Dixie's relationship had clear boundaries, caring, and respect, and appeared to have been without significant strain throughout their lives together. They truly blessed each other's lives, adjusting their roles as they grew older to allow and acknowledge each other's maturity and life experiences.

I should have known that just as she loved her mother so well in life, Donna would use that love to transform her experience of adjusting to Dixie's death. This book, which she began writing almost as soon as she returned from the funeral, is both the result and the beginning. In it, you will come to know two remarkable women.

Joan Matthews, Ph.D.

Acknowledgments

Several people made the writing of this book much easier because of their ongoing supportive feedback. My son, Wes Simonds, deserves special thanks. A writer himself, he read each section as I wrote it, gave me his personal reactions and very gentle suggestions, and provided support throughout the publication process. Every writer should have a son like Wes.

Betty Fry read, applauded, and gave suggestions throughout the first draft of this book. Earl Koile and Carol Lou Treat also provided ongoing feedback and encouragement. Joan Matthews read aloud to me each section she found especially appealing—what a trip! In addition, thanks go to Christy Gay, Linda Mulder, Bubba and Dixie Lee, Michael Duffy, Melba Vasquez, Phil McLarty, Mike Watkins, and Ken Gibble for reading various drafts and letting me know what touched them. My editor, Karen DeVinney, provided both professional and personal support during the review and publication of the manuscript.

My very deepest appreciation goes to those patients who, over the years, have honored me with their trust and have allowed me to be a companion in their pain, their struggles, their triumphs, and their creativity. You have each written your own song, and those melodies are deep in my heart and, in various ways, woven throughout this book.

Finally, in honor of the marvelous work done by not-for-profit Hospices, I am donating ten percent of my royalties to Hospice Brazos Valley.

Introduction

In early March, 1999, Mom said that she needed my help getting her affairs in order so that she could die. I spent that week dreading the task, and by the time I got to Dallas the next weekend, I felt like I was underwater. Sounds were muffled, the colors and spaces seemed distorted, and I kept hearing my own heartbeat. All I could focus on was the sadness and disbelief that had newly invaded the world where I lived.

Saturday at noon I drove over to a McDonald's. I had hoped that salty fries and catsup might restore some sense of normalcy, but I couldn't eat them. I sat at the table, fighting tears and reducing several paper napkins to tiny pieces—only slightly aware of the teenage boy sweeping around my table. "How ya doin'?" he asked, and I glanced up briefly to say I was fine. "No," he shook his head slowly. He took a step toward me and rested his hand on my table. Bending forward to look in my eyes, he said, "You look sad. I'm sorry."

Grief sometimes builds unexpected bridges. It feels a little strange not to know what you, the reader, may be going through in your life or why you have picked up this book. In the hope, though, that perhaps my story may help—or even build a bridge between us—I invite you to share with me the last year of my mother's life.

As a psychologist, I knew a good deal about grief going into this process. One of the things I verified for myself at a very personal level was that it is far from an orderly and sequential process; in fact, the whole experience was unpredictable and a bit messy. I found myself moving from intense feelings to memories of family stories and then on to professional musings; I was tossed about willy-nilly in a storm largely out of my control. It is this process that I have tried to capture impressionistically in my writing—a shifting kaleidoscope of feelings and thoughts and associations triggered by the impending loss of my much-loved mother.

It may help to understand a few things about our family. I've provided a family tree to clarify the varied relationships I refer to.

Family legacy, transmitted through stories, was important to Mom, and later to me; perhaps you will find as you read this that your own legacy will take on added meaning for you.

Mom moved to Dallas in 1993, having chosen a retirement village that offered three levels of care; she said she wanted to make this her last home. She lived there in a rented independent "cottage" except when she needed nursing care, at which times she moved over to the skilled nursing wing about one hundred yards away on the same grounds.

My brother Everard, called "Bubba" by me all my life, is an attorney in Dallas, where Mom was living. I teach at Texas A&M University, 173 miles southeast from Dallas, and my sister, Dixie Lee, lives in a little town another 125 miles southeast of me. In the months of Mom's final decline, my brother saw her almost every day, I spent every weekend with her, and Dixie Lee came less often but stayed longer. We siblings became a family team, trying to support each other and work together to help Mom. Most of the time, we succeeded.

A word about the format of the book: The personal memoir about my last year with my mother comes next. If you are interested in a more academic understanding of grief, you'll probably also want to read the last two chapters on anticipatory and post-bereavement grief.

Family Tree

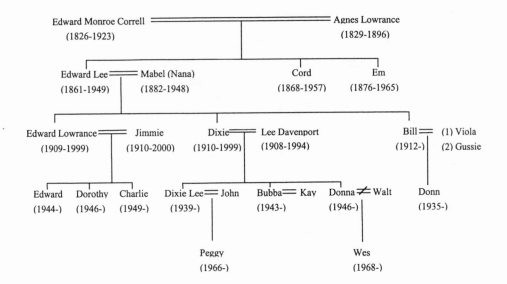

Edward Monroe Correll (1826-1923) ═══ Agnes Lowrance (1829-1896)

Edward Lee (1861-1949) ═══ Mabel (Nana) (1882-1948)   Cord (1868-1957)   Em (1876-1965)

Edward Lowrance (1909-1999) ═══ Jimmie (1910-2000)   Dixie (1910-1999) ═══ Lee Davenport (1908-1994)   Bill (1912-) ═══ (1) Viola / (2) Gussie

Edward (1944-)   Dorothy (1946-)   Charlie (1949-)   Dixie Lee (1939-) ═══ John   Bubba ═══ Kay (1943-)   Donna (1946-) ≠ Walt   Donn (1935-)

Peggy (1966-)   Wes (1968-)

Staying Connected through the Loss

When I was in elementary school, we lived in a small Texas town without a Presbyterian church so we attended the Methodist. If I was exposed to any theology, I don't remember it—except for recalling one Sunday School teacher who alluded to the dangers of backsliding. I must have expressed a lack of interest in the concept because my usually gentle teacher said with an edge to her voice, "Maybe you should think more about being saved, Donna Sue."

"No," I answered. "I don't need to. Mother will die before I do and *she* will be in heaven. If they won't let me in, she'll talk to God about it. I'll be okay."

That early certainty of Mom's ultimate destination, and my conviction that her love for me would keep me safe, did not diminish much for me over the years. I told her a few months before she died about this Sunday School exchange, only half-laughing at my younger self. She listened and smiled. She did not contradict me.

The family Christmas celebration in 1997 was at my house, and we have a videotape of Mother recounting early family history, recalling names, dates, stories, without a pause for recollection. My mother's love of family had blossomed into full-blown genealogical scholarship after retirement, and these people she talked about were very real to her. It was no effort for her to remember important information about people she loved, even if they had lived 150 years before.

The year 1998 had started off pretty well for Mother. After recovering from a bout of food poisoning the previous September, she had made it through the winter with no health problems. October of 1998 was Mom's last healthy month. By the end of it, she had been diagnosed with temporal arteritis and was on massive doses of Prednisone, which did curb the inflammation, but also led to disastrous weakness from which she could not recover.

But before that, in mid-October, she and my brother joined me for a few days in New England, where I was on sabbatical. One of my favorite memories of that trip is meeting them in the Boston airport. Their plane had been delayed several hours in its departure from Dallas and I expected that she would be very tired; I was thankful my brother was flying with her so she wouldn't have to deal with all the details by herself. I had the rental car available, and had made reservations for our night's lodging.

Finally the arrival of their flight was announced. Mom and Bubba were the last two passengers to deplane. As they came into the gate area, Mom in a wheelchair with my brother pushing, I walked toward them. Mother was wearing a brightly colored wool suit, a beautiful contrast to her silver hair. The instant she saw me, a delighted smile lit up her face. Her eyes were dancing and she threw open her arms for a hug. She could hardly wait to begin the week's adventures!

The leaves were dazzling. We meandered through Massachusetts, New Hampshire, and Vermont in our rental car, stopping to explore cemeteries, admire waterfalls and covered bridges, visit historical sites. Mother's headaches, it turned out, were beginning the last day or two of that trip, but she did not tell us. She immersed herself in the beauty of the scenery, sometimes wishing, I am sure, that she had her oil paints and a few canvases with her. Pictures of her taken on that trip show her with her glorious smile, wearing her signature bright colors, and with only a small deviation from her characteristic perfectly erect posture—a slight stoop required by the cane she used when she was walking. She was eighty-eight, glowing with pleasure and as beautiful and serene as she had always been.

The trip is memorable not only because it was her last one, but also because it was the only time I saw Mom show off. We had stopped to take pictures of some of the brilliantly colored trees in a cemetery in New Hampshire, and Mother was wandering around looking at tombstones. As we reached the rear area, she turned to me and said, "Go around to the other side of that stone." Slightly bewildered, I did as she asked. "Okay. Now I'm going to tell you the date of death within five years. 1780!" She was right; the date was 1783. Her excursions into family history had obviously included learning quite a lot about styles and shapes of tombstones across the generations.

She and my brother returned to Dallas and I came back at the end of the month. A few days before I left, I went to Virginia to visit her brother Ed. Uncle Ed seemed less jovial, more serious than usual. After about an hour of catching up, he said, "Your mother called. She wants you to call her before you leave." Something about the way he said it made me take a deep breath; it sounded serious. I placed the call immediately.

"What's going on, Mom? Is anything wrong?"

"Well, not much," she answered in a casual tone of voice. Very casual. "Just some funny test results they found when they tried to figure out why I was having headaches."

"I didn't know you'd been having headaches! How long? Why didn't you tell me?"

"Not too long, just a few weeks." *A few weeks?!* "I didn't want to worry you while you were on sabbatical. It's probably not serious anyway."

I tried to match her casual tone with my own. "Well, that's good. What do they think it is, anyway?"

"They call it temporal arteritis. It's just an inflammation of the arteries that go up to my temples. They put me on Prednisone and that's helping."

"Anything else, Mom?" Still appropriately nonchalant.

"Oh, just that they did biopsies on the sides of my face. It still hurts a little. It'll go away."

My uncle was studying my face, watching my reaction. This must be *really* serious.

"Okay. Well, it sounds like they're on top of it. So Prednisone will take care of it, huh?"

A pause. Then, "Well, doctor said he was hopeful. We'll see. See you next weekend?"

"Yep. I'll be there as soon as I pick up my car from the airport. About lunch time."

"I'll get them to make a plate for you in the dining room."

"Great. See you then."

I hung up and sat down. I looked at my uncle and he looked at me. The worry on his face must have been mirrored on my own, because he reached for my hand and said, "We're family, right? We're a team, all in this together! We'll handle it."

In the darkest place inside,
Something shuddered and took life.
Nothing quite so grand as
    a cataclysmic roar
    or a howl of anguish
    or even a whimper of fear.
Just a h-m-m-m, almost electronic,
    louder at night.

I will myself to ignore it,
I drown it out with music.
I distract myself, try to relax,
    focus on autumn's beauty.
It bides its time.
It whispers of sinister mystery,
    unnamed danger.
Finally, in anger and desperation
I demand—Make yourself known!

You are losing, you are losing her

My mother had been my rock, my anchor, the absolutely constant and trustworthy part of my life. We were not "best friends," as I've heard other women say of their mothers. I did not confide to her many important aspects of my life. We did not often discuss politics or social issues, although she knew that my views were far less conservative than hers. She had no real idea what my professional life was like.

Neither did it ever feel as if we had "switched roles," as some adult children say when speaking of their parents. On the surface, perhaps, I took on more protective behaviors as she grew more fragile with age. I arranged for airlines to have wheelchairs available; I shopped and cooked when I visited her on weekends; I (and my siblings) argued with nurses and doctors when the inevitable snafus occurred during her hospital stays. But she was no more dependent on me for advice than I was on her. She had a clear understanding of who she was and how she wanted to be, and that clarity gave her identity a sense of uncompromising integrity and strength.

She told me a story once of her and Dad's early married years. They were living in Corpus Christi, and my dad's father, a highly respected Texas Ranger who adored his new daughter-in-law, dropped by the house one day and suggested that she go someplace with him. My father said, when she told him, "Where did you go?"

She answered, "Well, we didn't. I told him I couldn't, that I had something else I had to do."

My father stared at her. "You told him no?"

"Yes, of course I told him no. We'll do it some other time."

"No one tells my father no."

"Well, I did, " she responded.

Telling me this story almost sixty years later, she said, "It never occurred to me I *couldn't* tell someone no! Of course I can!"

A couple of weeks after I returned to Texas, when Mom was still generally healthy, I got a call one night from Betty. Betty was the daughter of Mother's longtime friend Charles. She was asking me to let Mom know that her father had died quite unexpectedly that day in Albuquerque. I told Betty I would be driving into Dallas the next day and agreed to be the one to tell Mom.

As children, we grew up knowing that Charles had been one of my father's college roommates. They had stayed in touch over the years, and our two families visited each other a few times. Then in 1994, after my father and Charles' wife had died, Charles and Mom began writing to each other and talking on the phone. When Charles visited family in Austin, he made it a point to stop over to see Mom in Dallas. Somehow things caught fire. Mom finally mentioned nonchalantly that she and Charles had dated a bit in college before she met Dad. This was news!

It was fascinating for me to watch the renewal of their relationship. While the sexual energy was rather subdued, there was no doubt that there was a distinct male/female connection between the two of them. I was delighted that, well into their eighties, they could experience such feelings for each other. Mom's eyes lit up when she talked about Charles, and letters were responded to by return mail. One week I took Mom to New Mexico for a trip and chauffeured her and Charles around Santa Fe, trying to keep my eyes from drifting to the rearview mirror, lest I catch them snuggling in the back seat! I teased her a little about having a boyfriend. They apparently discussed his possible move to Dallas, and whether or not they should consider marriage.

So now, I was dreading having to tell her of Charles' death. Driving up to Dallas on Friday evening, I rehearsed various ways to break the news. None of them felt adequate.

By the time I reached her cottage, it was dark. All of her livingroom lights were turned on in anticipation of my arrival, and I walked in to see her smiling up at me from her recliner. We chatted for about fifteen minutes, catching up and laughing as we always did when we got back together. My internal voice kept telling me that I couldn't postpone giving her the news indefinitely. But it was very hard to bring it up. She was so happy, not knowing. I hated taking that away from her.

Finally there was a pause.

"Mom, I'm afraid I have some bad news. I got a call from Betty yesterday."

Mother grew very still. She looked at me and waited.

"Charles was showing his house to a real estate agent yesterday afternoon and he had a heart attack. It was very serious. They got him to the hospital, but couldn't save him. He died late afternoon. I'm so sorry."

Mom was quiet, trying to absorb it. She eventually asked a few questions about how I'd heard, when the funeral would be, how Betty was taking it.

It looked like she might want a little time alone, so I brought in my suitcase from the car and unpacked. After awhile I went back in her livingroom. She was still sitting there motionless, without tears. We sat in silence for awhile.

It was hard to tell exactly what she was feeling. I broke the silence.

"Does it ever get easier, hearing that someone has died? After you've lost a lot of family and friends, do you find a way to handle it? Maybe pray for them? Or do you somehow know that they are okay and does that help?"

Mom looked at me sadly. "No, it doesn't get easier. Each time it feels like a big hole in my chest, where something was ripped out. It doesn't get easier."

There were long years between generations on my mother's side of the family. Her grandfather, born in 1826, fought in the Civil War (War of Northern Aggression, my Aunt Cord would have said) and was flagbearer for Stonewall Jackson. Surely more influential to the family legacy, however, was the training in music he received in Philadelphia before the War. His parents were not wealthy. One can only assume that he had considerable talent to warrant their sending young Edward Monroe Correll so far from their small farm in North Carolina.

Edward M. wrote no memoirs and family history is sketchy that far back. We know few things about him—most of these related to music. We know he was choirmaster at two neighboring churches in North Carolina. We know he taught all of his children to sing, emphasizing harmony and enunciation. One letter saved from a neighbor during the 1880s alludes to the local teenagers' gathering at the Correll house on Sunday evenings for a supper of milk and bread—its being Sunday, after all, and not a time for extravagance—and then singing late into the evening, just for the joy of singing.

My grandfather, Edward Lee, was Edward M.'s child with the most musical training. In addition to singing and composing songs, he learned to play the guitar and the violin—and was taught the banjo by a beloved former slave who refused to leave the place after the War. "Uncle Frank," my grandfather called the old man. He wrote a spiritual in Uncle Frank's honor, the chorus of which goes:

> *I'm going home*
> *No more to roam*
> *I'm going to my abode.*
> *I'm going home*
> *Heaven is my home,*
> *I'm going up glory road.*

This chorus is the first recorded mention in our family of "home" being the after-life destination. It was this chorus that I sang most often to my mother—Edward Lee's daughter, Dixie—one night as she lay dying some 120 years after her father left Uncle Frank for Texas adventures.

❦

The family gathering at Thanksgiving of 1998 was at a niece's house in Austin. Mother and I shared a motel room that Thursday night. The worst side effect of the Prednisone was the weakness that it caused, and Thanksgiving was the first time that Mom was too weak to rise from a chair. I helped her up and we ignored the implications. Friday we drove to Bryan listening to the University of Texas/ Texas A&M football game on the radio, Mom cheering for the University of Texas. as she had every year since she entered as a freshman there seventy years before. When we got home, we watched the very satisfying last quarter on TV and then took naps. Later in the afternoon, I checked my email.

Betty had written, telling about the service for her dad and offering me some advice. *Talk with your mother while she's still healthy about how she wants her funeral.* I wasn't at all sure that Mother cared to do this, but I told her what Betty had said. As well as I could read her reaction, she seemed to indicate a grudging willingness.

"Do you have any special instructions about how you want your funeral, Mom? What do you want to wear?"

"Oh, I guess something white. I've got the long white dress I made years ago; it opens down the back and should be easy to get me into."

An image of Mother in a casket arose unbidden in my mind, and tears came to my eyes. My throat tightened. This would not do. It was too sad; I'd never get through it.

"Let's do this a little differently. I'll tell you what I want, in case I die first, and you tell me what you want. I want to be buried in bright red. Red shoes, too."

Mom smiled a little. "Honey, I don't think they have shoes in the casket."

I was disappointed. I'd dabbled with the possibility of slipping red shoes on Mom, too—unnoticeable to anyone, but nonetheless making a statement to eternity about Mom's identity.

"Yes," she resumed. "We'll go with white. I thought once I might want to wear my wedding dress, but I guess that's not appropriate." Her wedding dress was a long velvet dress, wine colored, that she had chosen in honor of her Christmas Day wedding. After letting it out when, to her chagrin, her waistline ballooned after three babies from twenty-two and one-half inches to twenty-four inches, she had worn the dress several times, the last at her and Dad's fiftieth anniversary dinner.

"Okay. Red for me, white for you. I wanted to keep your wedding dress anyway, if that's all right. Do you want to wear any jewelry?"

She looked a little shocked. "Oh, no! You *don't* bury jewelry!"

"Glasses?"

"Whatever you children decide is fine with me."

"What about the service itself? Do you want a memorial service at the Village?"

"No, they don't allow it. I guess just a short service at the church."

The conversation continued in this pleasantly speculative way, and we discussed songs we each wanted, charities we wanted contributions to go to, flowers, and the like for about fifteen minutes.

As I fell asleep later, I congratulated myself on our getting through a difficult discussion with relative ease. I thought of a couple of more questions I needed to ask before she left for Dallas.

The next morning I asked how she had slept, expecting her usual upbeat answer. Instead she shook her head and said a little grumpily, "Not too good. I dreamed about bodies and caskets all night!" Thus ended that discussion.

By mid-December, the weakness caused by the Prednisone had worsened. She moved from her cottage to a skilled nursing wing of the retirement village. She began forgetting things and she developed the "moon face" characteristic of steroid use. I looked up Prednisone in my Physicians Desk Reference, and it included all these side effects, plus other terrible ones. We told her and ourselves that when she could cut back, she would improve and return to her cottage. In the meantime, the anxiety inside me increased. *Do something. Fix this now.*

※

Mom was born in El Campo, Texas, on August 13, 1910. Her dad was twenty-one years older than her mother, forty-seven to her twenty-six, when they were married. (The story goes that when he told *his* father, Edward M., that he planned to marry, his father pondered a minute and then said solemnly, "Well, it's time you were about it.")

The life of Edward Lee, my grandfather, is a bit of a mystery. We know he left North Carolina to come to Texas in the early 1880s. We know he rode with the Texas Rangers for awhile, and then settled down in the Ft. Worth/Dallas area where he managed several large hotels, still only a young man in his twenties.

Then he was in Mexico—perhaps managing a hotel. Rumor is that he killed a man and was ordered to stay in the city by Mexican authorities. By this time his parents and siblings had transplanted themselves from North Carolina to south Texas. When Edward Lee received word that his mother was dying of cancer, he returned to Texas, apparently eluding any Mexican officials trying to pursue him. After returning, he stayed, settling in a small south Texas town where he established the ice house, served on the volunteer fire department, was twice elected mayor—and later Justice of the Peace—and owned a meat market. He met and married my grandmother, Mabel George, and together they raised their family of three children.

Mabel, "Nana," as her children and grandchildren called her, was a governess when they met. They apparently had a very loving relationship. (He used to joke, however, when asked to what he attributed his long life, that when he and Mabel got married, they agreed that if they had a squabble he would go off for a long walk and she would prepare his favorite supper. "It was all that good food and exercise," he would say, that kept him young.) He was very protective of Nana, determined to keep his pre-nuptial promise not to let her down by dying before she did. He kept his promise.

Dixie, my mom, was the much-loved middle child, the only girl and the apple of her father's eye; she was his Gal-baby. Blessed not only with loving parents, but also with a sunny disposition, she had a bright, inquisitive mind and radiated a quiet confidence. She grew up and married in the house where she was born. Much later, after she retired and began oil painting, she did a painting of this house, calling the picture "Home."

When she gave me an oil transfer of the painting, she told me a story that took place in each room of the house, including the front porch and stairway. I learned that her two-year-old brother, upon leaving his candy on the porch and having their St. Bernard eat it, yelled "My tandy! My tandy! " and put his hand down the obliging dog's throat to get it back. The diningroom was where my grandfather waited, a pistol hidden under a newspaper, for the KKK to retaliate for his publishing information about its membership and tactics. The downstairs bedroom was where Mom's favorite aunt recuperated from having an arm crushed during a tornado, an event which had taken the life of her mother, her husband, and her two sons. Mom's painting fairly vibrated with loving memories and associations.

Once, a few years before she died, she and I drove through El Campo and stopped by where her house had been. She had known that the house itself had burned, but was pleased that a present dwelling was resting on the old foundation. As she sat there, lost in memories, the door opened and an unkempt fellow, beer gut hanging over his shorts and carrying a beer can, sauntered out. He asked what we wanted. Mother lowered her window, smiled pleasantly, and began telling him that her parents had moved into the house that had originally been there on their wedding day and that she had been born there. The fellow shifted his weight and drank some beer. Mom explained where a gardenia bush had been, how there had been a sleeping porch upstairs, and how she used to play in a tree in the side yard. She told him when they had installed indoor plumbing and who the neighbors were. By now, the man was uncomfortable. How was he going to get out of this?

Mom was in the process of describing the floor plan when a woman appeared in the doorway. "Hank?" she yelled. "Everything okay?"

Mother smiled at her, nodded, and continued her explanation, raising her voice just slightly to refocus Hank on what she was saying. She told him about the outhouse, where the barn had been, where the clothesline was. Hank looked trapped, clearly over his head. He stared at his empty beer can and shifted from foot to foot. She told him about her brother practicing drop-kicks in the vacant yard next door, and Nana washing clothes in the back yard. I believe she mentioned when the sidewalk was put in. Finally, she let him go.

As she was fastening her seat belt, I said, "You know, Mom, I'm not sure he really wanted to hear all that." She nodded in agreement.

"Why did you tell him when he didn't want to know?"

She looked at me. "He *needed* to know."

Virtually all of Mom's memories that she shared with us—even the sad ones—were set in this context of a safe, secure childhood. Home to her was this house, but it was also El Campo, the small town on the Texas coastal plains where everyone knew and respected her father, where she was cheerleader and debater and valedictorian, and where her parents died and were buried. Later, she and my dad lived on the Mexico border in Del Rio for thirty-two years and called it home, but in the last months of her life, when she referred to "home," it meant El Campo.

Home thus encompassed not only where you were going after you died, but also where you were from, where you were rooted. Home was where you were supported by love.

We had planned Christmas of 1998 to be at my brother's house in Dallas, with his children and their families, my sister and her family, and me and my son driving in from out of town. Mother was to be released from the nursing unit during the days of the 24th and 25th, to return there at night. We were looking forward to being all together for the first time since my father had died in 1994. Christmas was my mom's favorite time of year, and we wanted this occasion to be perfect for her.

The worst ice storm in decades hit Texas on December twenty-third. My son, Wes, due to fly in from California, had his flight delayed, and most of the state's roadways became impassible. Family phones worked overtime as we tried to devise alternate plans, revised them when the road conditions didn't improve, and finally limped into Dallas in various assorted groups. Wes's plane finally arrived in Austin at one A.M. Christmas morning; we were able after a couple of hours' sleep to arrive at my brother's about eleven o'clock. I tried not to be too annoyed that the weather had cheated me out of a whole day of family fun.

Mom was happy, but very weak, and exhausted by the end of Christmas day. I had forgotten my camera in the chaos of leaving home, but I have strong memories of Mother smiling, but growing quieter and quieter as the day went on. It felt to me that, like a rubber band that has been stretched too many times, her resiliency was almost worn out. Reassurances I gave myself felt hollow, and although I tried to dismiss as overly dramatic my inner certainty that this would be her last Christmas, I could not shake the undercurrent of sadness that followed me all day.

❧

For my Christmas present from Mother, I received an ecru table cloth, crocheted many years before by my mother's Aunt Cord, Edward Lee's sister. Aunt Cord was a legend in the family. Forbidden by her father to marry when she was young because as the oldest daughter it was her responsibility to take care of him, she had lived in poverty with the dreaded title of "old maid." Nonetheless, no one dared feel sorry for her. My mother's posture was erect, but it suffered in comparison with Aunt Cord's military bearing.

Anne Cordelia Linn Correll was a staunch Presbyterian; while some Presbyterians of that generation began softening a bit from their Calvinistic roots, you got the feeling that Aunt Cord might want to take Calvin aside and speak to him firmly about being so wishy-washy. She tithed, of course—ten per cent of her income *before* taxes. She walked out of a church service only once that we know of, when a woman dared to make an announcement standing behind the pulpit. Mother's brother Ed used to tell the story of Aunt Cord's visit to El Campo one weekend when he was a young boy. Just after World War

I, barnstorming airplanes occasionally flew over and landed in a field close to their house. One Sunday at dinner an airplane rumbled overhead, and forgetting to excuse himself, my uncle dashed outside to watch. Aunt Cord was hot on his heels with a reprimand. As she drew breath to begin, she looked up to see the airplane pilot doing stunts— flips and dives and barrel rolls. Stunned by such foolery, Aunt Cord scowled, raised her finger, and shouted at the pilot, "Thou shalt not *tempt* the Lord, thy God!"

Another story of Aunt Cord that I had not heard until recently: She and her sister, Aunt Em, were walking to town in the 1920s— Aunt Em strolling, Aunt Cord impatient—down the middle of the road. An automobile, still fairly rare at that time in this small town, approached. Aunt Em hurried to the side of the road; Aunt Cord raised her chin and continued advancing. At the last minute, Em tackled her and knocked her into the ditch. Outraged, Aunt Cord stood and brushed herself off. "Why, may I be so bold as to ask, would you do that?" "Cord, that car would have *hit* you. You're supposed to get out of the way!" "Well, I disagree," Aunt Cord sniffed. "I pay taxes for this road also."

Aunt Em moved in with Aunt Cord after her husband died. Cord must have made a formidable roommate for her gentler sister Em. As a child I once witnessed the two elderly, very deaf sisters arguing, Aunt Em finding it difficult to counter Cord's righteous Biblical allusions to Truth. Finally, with a certain flair, Em glared at her sister and in an act of unmistakable provocation reached up and turned off her hearing aid.

While I was pleased, then, to receive the beautifully crocheted tablecloth for a Christmas present, at that point my positive associations were because it had been my mom's, not really because Aunt Cord had made it. Why Mother felt close to her was a mystery to me. I admired Cord's strength of character, but saw no trace of the warmth that other members of the Correll family were known for.

❧

January was a month for us of only cautious hope. As she had after other medical difficulties, Mother began physical therapy. This time, however, was very different from the previous occasions. She worked as hard, if not harder, but was discouraged by how slowly she made progress. She was still on a very high dosage of Prednisone, and its devastating effects continued to try to sweep her downstream. By this point the drug was also beginning to affect her personality in small but noticeable ways. She, up until now so optimistic, was a bit irritable in a manner that was incompatible with her values and history. There had been one episode just before Christmas of her believing something had happened which had not. It took us all aback; we had relied all our lives on the accuracy and breadth of Mom's memory. How could this be happening?

The last weekend in January we got permission for Mom to go back to the cottage, under my care, to see if she could function there. I did the shopping and cooking and cleaning, helped with her dressing and bathing, and kept the place straight. Using all of her energy, she was able to get up and down from bed and from her recliner, make it back and forth to the bathroom with a walker, and do her physical therapy activities. Her vision was blurred because of the Prednisone, but she was too exhausted to read anyway. Still, she was so glad to be back in the cottage that she and I agreed that with someone there during the day, she would (barely) be able to resume living there, rather than the nursing unit.

Sunday night, after she had gotten into her pajamas, taken out her hearing aids, and was ready for bed, she came back into the livingroom with her walker. She was looking for something. Knowing how tired she was, I wanted to do the looking for her. Without the aids, she couldn't hear a word I said, so I gestured, *What are you looking for?*

"I can't find my 'reacher'," she said. The reacher was a gadget with a gripper at one end and a scissor-like handle on the other, designed to help people reach objects without getting up or bending over. I looked in the only three rooms where she had been, and found one in the bathroom. I brought it to her.

"No!" she said irritably. "Not that one. I need the metal reacher, not that cheap plastic one."

Surprised at her tone, I raised my eyebrows but kept looking. I looked under her bed, behind and under the sofa, under bookcases. The cottage wasn't that big; there were few places for things to hide. I couldn't find it. I looked in the kitchen, thinking maybe she went in there with it when I had taken a nap. It was nowhere. Knowing she couldn't hear me, I wrote her a note: *Could you have left it over at the nursing unit?*

"No!" she barked. "I know I had it here! I used it this morning!"

She had snapped like that at me maybe three times in my adult life. I wasn't pleased to be the recipient of that tone of voice now, when I was trying to help. I shrugged and went back to the sofa and picked up my book. After a few more minutes of looking, she went to bed.

She was in a better mood the next day and neither of us mentioned the incident.

That afternoon I had to take her back over to the nursing unit to spend the night before they would release her. Policy: Patients can only be released when they are physically occupying a room. Okay, whatever. It made no sense, but it wasn't worth arguing over. Someone else would have to go back over to get her the next day, but my sister, Dixie Lee, was coming up anyway to stay for a few days, so she could tend to the details of the move.

I got Mom settled, unpacked her belongings, made sure the kitchen knew to serve her meals through the next day. Just before I left to make the drive back home, I looked under the bed. There was the metal reacher. I was torn between an unbecoming urge to show it to her so she would know I'd been right the night before, and the desire to help her save face by putting it somewhere accessible that she would see after I left. As I moved to put it on her bedside table, she turned around to say something to me and saw it in my hand.

"Oh, good. Where did you find it?"

"It was under the bed."

"Okay, as long as it's found."

I told her I was a little worried that she had been so clear about using it the day before. I didn't mention any of the psychological explanations for her mistake—none of them was reassuring—but I did say that Prednisone can cause such memory loss. As I drove home, I chastised myself for saying anything. What had been the point? Did I expect her to somehow comfort me?

She told Bubba the next day what had happened, and mentioned that I had said I was worried. He reassured her that I probably worried too easily about such things and the subject did not come up again.

❧

The power of Prednisone to make Mom's life so difficult and to diminish her presence felt personal and offensive to me. Anger at the drug allowed for some small focus of my anxiety and made me feel better. I was offended, really offended, that my mother, who had tried so hard, should suffer such assault. Medical science had nothing else to offer her: Prednisone was the best alternative to address the arteritis. My sense of outrage and sadness that who she *was* was somehow being taken away piece by piece, in spite of her determination to hold on, left me emotionally exhausted. I wanted very badly to fight, and the lack of a tangible enemy was indescribably frustrating.

Dixie Lee, my sister, stayed with Mother during the first few days of February, and then one of her daughters, Peggy, offered to come stay with Mom while we waited to see if she could live independently again. Peggy was an R.N. recovering from a knee operation, so her willingness to come was a wonderful solution from the family's point of view. She moved in, and with the help of occasional sitters, Mom was able to live for one more month in her own cottage.

❧

I was there every weekend so that Peggy could leave town and have some fun. I had taken up a folding bed so I could sleep in Mom's room, but the mattress sagged in the frame and was too hard on the floor. Finally it occurred to me to get a room monitor, which allowed whoever was there to sleep in the other bedroom and still hear her if she called.

One Saturday night about two A.M., the speaker beside my bed woke me up. Mother was singing. "Wake up, wake up, my daughter dear! I need some help getting up from here!"

I went to her room and helped her swing her legs over the side of the bed, and using her walker, she slowly made her way to the bathroom. Since she insisted on walking without my help, she moved very slowly; I knew it would take her at least ten minutes to return. Still half asleep, I lay down in her bed and pulled up the blanket to wait. I must have dozed off. When I opened my eyes, she was standing by the bed, supporting herself with the walker.

She looked amused.

"Keeping my bed warm for me?"

I helped her get back in bed, arranged the pillows the way she liked, and pulled up her new pink blanket. As I tucked in the blanket around her shoulders, I had a memory flash of many childhood nights when she had lovingly done the same for me. I kissed her on the forehead and then straightened. She was looking at me, and we shared a certainty of knowing that we were thinking the same thing. With her hearing aids out, she could not hear me, but we smiled at each other and nodded in acknowledgement.

It was not, I thought, that we had changed roles. We had simply changed behaviors. She was still the mother, I the daughter. Nothing essential had changed. The difference was that these circumstances gave me the opportunity to return some of the tenderness I had received from her over the years.

The light coming from the bathroom was dim, but bright enough that I could see colors. Lying on her back, Mom looked young again, and peaceful; the puffiness and wrinkles in her face had disappeared. The image has lingered in my mind: Pink blanket and spun silver hair, surrounding her beautiful face. It was one of those moments of undeniable connection when thoughts and love were shared effortlessly. It was as if things were still normal.

By the end of February, it was clear that the January progress Mom had made was slipping away. She was too weak to keep up with physical therapy, she had another episode of believing something had happened which had not, and she had a couple of brief spells when she was disoriented, incontinent, and angry—after which she was much weaker. We hypothesized small strokes; somehow oxygen just wasn't getting to her brain all the time.

We moved her back to the nursing unit in March and in spite of continued physical therapy, except for emergency trips to the hospital, she never left her room again.

❦

In graduate school in the 1970s, one of the things we psychology students did was figure out how our parents had messed us up. One should be charitable about these judgments, it was understood, but nonetheless able to trace certain aspects of our current "dysfunctions" to the lack of appropriate parenting. It was especially trendy to find the mother to blame. So in spite of our burgeoning feminism, conversations took place informally about various maternal deficiencies that we had experienced. Most students could talk specifically and at length on this topic.

I was very quiet during these discussions. It was embarrassing: I couldn't think of very many flaws in Mom. She hadn't been depressed, or too weak, or too controlling when I was growing up. I couldn't find evidence of authority issues, clinging demands, or competition. Almost always she was supportive of my goals and interested in what my life was like. The most disapproving she had been in years was when I told her I was going to do my dissertation on either sexual orientation or death. She had crinkled her brow and said, "Honey, couldn't you find something more *uplifting* to do research on?" That was hardly worth contributing to these discussions of maternal inadequacies!

Several years later, after I graduated, I spent a week at my folks' house in Del Rio. One afternoon I was on the porch swing, reading a book, and Mother came out and sat down beside me. I closed my book so we could talk.

"I have an agenda for this trip," I said to her. I watched her take a second to brace herself so she would be prepared. Would I announce that I was pregnant? Would I say I was moving to a foreign country, never to return? Would I disclose that I had done my dissertation on lesbian relationships because *I* was gay? Whatever, in a second she was ready for it.

"I say really good things about you all the time to other people, and I thought recently that you don't know what I say. I want you to know. So I'm going to tell you some things, and you're supposed to sit there and listen. You shouldn't interrupt or change the subject!"

She narrowed her eyes, not at all sure she wanted this. Bad news, she could handle. But a series of compliments?

I mentioned her strength and her warmth before she tried to change the subject. *I'm teary, you're teary, let's move on!* was her signal.

I ignored her. I told her that I was proud that she had taken up oil painting after retirement and that she was currently taking sign language classes. I told her I loved that she always exuded a quiet vitality. I mentioned that I admired her graciousness with others, her consistent support for family, her quiet strength and courage.

By now she was noticeably uncomfortable, ready to get up.

I summarized a few more points, told her that I had always wished I had her self-discipline and her ability to accept difficult times with so much grace. I gave a few examples, and then I let her go. I didn't say all I planned to, but I think she got the message: I thought that, as a human being, she was terrific! I was glad I'd made her listen, even if it made her uncomfortable. I needed her to know.

❦

Charles had died in November, and then in late January Mom's beloved older brother Ed died. Back on the nursing unit in March, Mother told my brother that these were her wake-up calls: She could die at any time and needed to get her records and final plans in shape ASAP. Bubba called to tell me that Mom had said that she would need my help, but that she was worried that I didn't want to talk with her about her dying. She was right that I didn't want to, not at all, but I was a little miffed that I got no credit for having initiated the subject over Thanksgiving. She, who had the most marvelous memory, had forgotten. More of the ongoing effects of Prednisone.

As I drove to Dallas that weekend, thoughts tumbled through my head. How was I to help her die? How could I support her, help her, when every instinct inside cried, *No. This is **not** okay. **Stop this**. At once!* I recalled Dylan Thomas' plea to his dying father: Do not go gentle into that good night. Rage, rage against the dying of the Light! But I also told myself that the only way to remain connected with Mom was to support her agenda; I could not expect her to switch focus at this point. I reminded myself that I had learned over the years as a therapist how to step into patients' worlds to meet them in their process, and then after the session move back into my own. I told myself that, although it would be a lot more difficult, if I could do it for patients, I could certainly do it for Mom.

Wanting still to fix things, to make guarantees,
Or at least do these hard months for her,
I hear reality's thunder crash over my wishes.

The current is too strong,
I cannot save her.
There are rapids up ahead—
    whirlpools and undercurrents—
That will surely take her from me.

I hate it, I hate it.
I cry in the car, I kick a trashcan against the wall.
No surprise—my tears change nothing.
This process does not like me.
It clearly does not listen.

And so, a compromise of sorts,
    A promise:
I will stay with you,
You will not be alone.
Tell me what you need and I will help.
Tell me what you feel and I will understand.
And when you cannot tell me anymore,
When words no longer come,
When you cannot call across the chasm,
I will still be here.

That first weekend I was in tears every time I walked out of her room. It was very, very sad, and a bit surreal, to talk with her so matter-of-factly about her death. It made me feel a little light-headed. I found that I could put my own feelings and reactions on hold for about an hour; then the effort of doing that and still trying to remain believably authentic to her caused mounting internal stress. I made up various excuses to go back to the cottage, and so gave myself periods of time when I could cry, decompress, and recollect myself before going back to be with her.

We spent every weekend in March going through family letters, scrapbooks, clothes, and songs. I would go through file cabinets and drawers and bookcases and cedar chests in her cottage, find interesting family information, and take it over to her room in the nursing wing. Some weekends Mom was strong enough that we talked an hour or so, some only a few minutes. It meant a lot to her to do this, so I did it willingly but without a lot of enthusiasm. She was passing on the genealogy torch, and I hated the implications of that.

And then, unexpectedly, in spite of the grief I was experiencing, it all came alive for me. I'd always enjoyed listening to Mother relate family stories, but the enjoyment was primarily because it was fun watching her so involved and alive. Now I began to get a sense of how real people can be when you read letters written well over one hundred years ago, or hold a dress worn the day after someone's wedding in the 1850s. I found baby dresses Nana had made when my mother was a baby almost ninety years before with tiny, tiny stitches in the little tucks, hand sewn buttonholes, crocheted trim and embroidery lovingly added to the bodice. I also found baby clothes Mom had made for us over fifty years before: tiny morning dresses and christening gowns and sacques, stitched with the same loving care that her mother had demonstrated. I recalled the sacques Mother had made and imprinted that I, in turn, had embroidered for my expected baby thirty years before. The sense of family legacy became palpable. More, it provided surprising sustenance.

It was hard for me to describe the change that happened inside me. There was life—a kind of vibrant aliveness—emanating from these heirlooms. It was contagious. I could almost breathe it in, feel it enter my bloodstream. I understood now why many bereaved people keep a pillow or sweater a loved one had and sometimes bury their faces in it. These are not just "linking objects," as my profession refers to them; something essential seems to be just barely connected with. Mother was dying, and yet somehow these treasures she had saved for so long still transmitted her past vitality. Birth as the beginning of one's life and death as the end of it surely was an undeniable physical reality, but not, I was slowly sensing, the *only* reality.

I read letters saved over the generations: A letter to my great-great grandmother from her aunt in Ohio to hold on to the land in Texas, that Polk had been elected President and Texas was probably going to be annexed into the Union. There were love letters from one of my great-grandfathers to his wife of twenty years. Letters to one of Edward M.'s daughters from her suitor and future husband. More letters from my great-grandfather Edward M. to his sister, letters from my grandfather Edward Lee to his sister Cord, letters from Uncle Ed to Mother. I told my brother he'd better get busy writing lovely letters to me if he didn't want to be responsible for ending the tradition carried down through the generations.

We went through daguerreotypes and old family photographs collected from the mid-1800s. I discovered baby pictures of my father I had never seen and a letter written by my dad's mother to her niece on Dad's first birthday. I read the diary that Nana had kept as a teenager in the 1890s.

Mother told me stories I'd never heard before: My dad's mother had jilted her first fiance, deciding after wedding invitations had been mailed that she would rather marry my grandfather. I learned that Nana had never called my grandfather by his first name; he was "your father" to the children, "Mr. Correll" to anyone else, and "Sweets" when she addressed him personally. I heard a story about a Sunday School gathering that Mother attended her first week at the University of Texas. The young men and women were gathered at their teacher's house, and he teased Mom by asking which man she would choose as the best looking. Deciding that the only way to respond would be to joke, my mother looked around slowly and then said, "There's really not much to choose from, is there?"

I learned more about Aunt Cord. Mom had always insisted that Cord cared about people as deeply as Aunt Em but just showed it differently. Possibly, but I remembered Aunt Cord, and I was not convinced. Among the letters that Mother and I went through were cards mailed to Cord from France by two of her nephews and their friends during World War I. There was a box of letters to her from her Uncle Will Lowrance—founding pastor of Oak Cliff Presbyterian Church where Mother was now a member—letters that were chatty and affectionate. Aunt Cord had also saved Christmas postcards she had received during the early 1900s. There was a lace handkerchief someone had brought her from the 1905 World's Fair. The softer side of her that Mom had told me about became more visible to me now, many years past her death. I began to suspect that beneath her austerity may have run undercurrents of wistfulness and love, a longing to connect with others.

I thought back to my childhood conviction that Mom would be in heaven to look after my best interests if I had trouble getting in. I was pretty sure now that if push came to shove, I could count on my Aunt Cord to enter the fracas on my behalf, however much she might regret some of my behaviors.

🌂

Almost imperceptibly, I started to absorb more of Mom's understanding of heritage. I had seen her wrap herself in the tapestry of family legacy and draw from it much of the strength and grace by which she was known. I understood that she had a perspective seasoned by the many stories of integrity and love shown by her predecessors. And now I found that as I spent hours in the cottage going through things, and then listening to Mom talk about them when I took them to her room, I was unconsciously trying out this perspective for myself and deriving surprising comfort. The painful, bittersweet experience of trying to help Mother prepare to die was not diminished by this generational perspective; on the contrary, my sadness in the Spring of 1999 became part of the context, added to experiences of earlier family members who would have understood what I was feeling because they too had loved, lost, grieved, and gone on. What had started out as a favor for Mom had become a source of much-needed nourishment and perspective for me. We were of the same heritage, and nothing, *nothing*, could change that.

Words to a song I had heard Holly Near sing several years before flooded back. When I sang them to myself going and coming from Dallas I found that I was able to internalize them a bit:

> *But you're not really gonna leave me, . .*
> *It is your path I walk.*
> *It is your song I sing.*
> *It is your load I take on.*
> *It is your air I breathe.*
> *It's the record you set that makes me go on.*
> *It's your faith that helps me stand.*

Mom's concept of family had no overtones of submissiveness or deference; learning to trust your own judgment was expected as a component of family closeness. Once when we were talking about her early life, I asked her what it had been like for her, moving back to El Campo to support her parents during the Depression. Did she worry that she would never marry? No, she answered, she was not interested in marrying anyone anyway until my father came along. She paused. Then she said, "What I was afraid of was staying so long that I would feel trapped and would never leave." Was she thinking of Aunt Cord?

Mom was very clear that the job of parents was to see that their children were strong enough to make it without the parents' support. As she said, they are going to have to—someday—anyway. Accordingly, as our mother, she very rarely offered advice after we left home, never let us see a trace of unhappiness if we moved far away, never indicated even subtly that we owed her anything. She gave us life, she loved and guided us as children, and then she set us free.

❦

During March and April of 1999, as Mother and I went through all the family records, her health continued a rapid downward trajectory. Time seemed very limited. The doctor was able to cut back on the Prednisone, but new difficulties kept arising with terrible predictability. At various times Mother would run a fever, be unresponsive, and would eventually be diagnosed with another infection. Sometimes these were handled at the nursing home, sometimes it meant trips to the hospital. During one of these hospital stays they discovered blood clots in her legs, clots that they surmised had been reaching her lungs and causing the occasional periods of extreme disorientation, incontinence, and weakness. They inserted a kind of filter in the vena cava. Whether or not this was what prevented more of the strange disoriented spells, they did seem to diminish. On the other hand, her body, which had already been retaining fluid, now became even more swollen. Her pant size went from eight to ten to twelve to fourteen. Diuretics that had worked before had no influence at all.

It was getting harder for me to laugh. Nothing seemed very light or funny anymore. I could not stop the process happening to my mother and the despair resulting from that was seeping into the corners of my life.

I took a Tuesday afternoon off from work one day in March to shop for larger blouses and pants with elastic waists. It took awhile to find colors and styles I thought she would like. Although I would be going to Dallas as usual on Friday, I decided I would mail them so she would have the fun of opening a package. Offering her a little fun for a change was an inspiring idea. My imagination stirred. Maybe it was not too late. Maybe there was still something I could do to brighten her day. My brother's family had a yearly celebration of Christmas in July, and I decided to make this a Christmas in March package. Feeling an upsurge of hopefulness for the first time in months, I found Christmas wrapping for the box of clothes, baked Christmas cookies and put them in a bright holiday cookie tin, and added a Christmas card. I rushed to get the package to the post office before five o'clock and just made it.

Thursday morning I received a call that Mother was worse. I cancelled appointments and was in Dallas at noon when the mail arrived, my package included. Mother was too exhausted and sick to pretend excitement. Peggy helped her open the package.

A few days later, after Mom was feeling a bit better, she mentioned to Peggy that she needed some larger clothes. Peggy brought out the Christmas package from the closet and showed Mom the clothes I'd sent.

"Where did these come from?" Mother asked.

"Aunt Donna sent them, remember? You saw them on Thursday."

"I did? I don't remember. What's in the tin?"

"Christmas cookies, remember? It's a Christmas in March package!"

"Oh," was Mom's response.

I was losing the ability to add fun to my mother's life.

❦

A week later, the nursing home asked us to provide skirts that would be easier to manage over the diapers she now wore than the pants I had just bought. I found several skirts with elastic waistbands in department stores, and furnished more from my own closet. I went through her closet and my own to find blouses in larger sizes than she had been wearing. At the staff's insistence, she began wearing skirts split up the side and blouses on the outside of the skirt.

One weekend, when we had been trying to mix and match some presentable outfits, I left her room to return to the cottage feeling very discouraged. My mother, always dressed neatly and in striking colors, had never worn her shirttail out in her life. Her style of clothing matched her own personality of brightness and order. Now not only was she reduced to sloppy attire, she had given up caring. She had no energy to waste on cosmetic appearances. In some ways I was glad; I would have hated for her to have been ashamed of her current appearance. But it was another indication to me that she was losing ground, losing the battle to remain herself in the face of death.

Back at the cottage, I went through her closet. Many of the clothes there I had bought her over the last several years, and I paused to touch each piece. I'm not sure what I thought I would accomplish in that closet, but it brought on the strongest single wave of grief I was to experience until the weeks just before her death. My hand moved to the purple jogging suit, the turquoise dress, the mint green suit. Something inside me gave way. Holding her bright red wool coat in my arms, I sobbed, giving up this symbol of the mother I had always known. What I wanted for her had become clearly unrealistic. There was no doubt: She would never again wear these clothes, never return to independent living, never walk, never be able to turn over in bed.

❦

Mom and I had talked over the years about death, in story form, naturally. Her first experience with death was when a classmate died in the second or third grade. She told me the story once: At first it didn't seem at all real. She had no idea what death was, no comprehension of its finality. The drama of the situation seemed very much like a make believe game.

The tradition back then in this small Texas town was to bring flowers from home gardens to the funeral, so that morning Mother happily went from house to house getting permission to cut their gardenias. She and her parents went to the church, she with her bouquet of flowers, looking forward with excitement to whatever was going to happen.

It was nothing like she expected: Her friend's body was in a casket. Grownups she thought never cried were in tears. The minister tried to offer solace through his own obvious dismay. As the service progressed, the seriousness of what had happened began to seep in. The word "never" took on new meaning for her: She would never, ever see her playmate again. They would not play together at recess, or share secrets, or practice spelling words together.

Then, as she and her parents were leaving the church, she in tears and holding onto her parents' hands for comfort, the mother of the deceased playmate came up to her.

"Are you Dixie?"

Mom couldn't answer, but she nodded.

"Mary wanted me to tell you goodbye for her."

I knew that the night my father died, my mother had been in to see him. He was asleep, and for the first time in fifty-six years, did not rouse when she kissed his forehead. She told me she sat beside his bed and looked at him, saw how very sick he was, and began to pray for him. She paused in her prayer to ask herself if she could tell God that it would be all right to take him. After a struggle with herself, she said she was able to let him go, to leave the decisions about him in God's hands. She bent over to kiss his forehead and moved toward the door, then turned again to come back to kiss him once more. Walked back to the door, and returned again for one last kiss.

It was upsetting but not surprising to her when the call came two hours later that he had died.

I had heard about Mom being by her mother's side as she lay dying. Mom had been summoned to come quickly, and was in El Campo within hours. Nana was unconscious, breathing lightly, apparently in no pain. Mother watched as Nana's breathing slowed: fifteen breaths, then a pause, fourteen breaths, then a pause—down until her last breath and then an easy slipping into death. Mother said she was greatly comforted by the fact that Nana's face seemed increasingly peaceful and youthful, until by the end, she looked like the Nana that Mom remembered from her childhood.

Another incident, which actually preceded death by a few days, I witnessed. Aunt Em, by then in her 90's, had been taken unconscious to the hospital in Edna. I was in college, but somehow got free to accompany Mother to see her. Aunt Em had had no children, and Mom, as her favorite niece, sometimes filled that role. We found Aunt Em's hospital room, and went in to see if she was conscious. She looked asleep to me, and I was hesitant to waken her. Mother, though, sat on the hospital bed beside her, took her hand in both of hers, and called, "Aunt Em, it's Dixie. It's Dixie, Aunt Em. Can you hear me? It's Dixie." She continued for about five minutes, with no response from Aunt Em. Mom remained calm, but I felt tears welling.

Part of what underlay my tears was the participation for the first time in a process which would clearly and inevitably lead to death. Aunt Em had not yet officially died, but she was no longer available to those who loved her. More, though, I think my tears were for Mom. It would have meant so much to her for Aunt Em to have responded even a little bit, to have had one more time to connect before the final separation.

The death that I had heard about since childhood was of Mother's father, Edward Lee. He was in his late eighties and had been making one of his twice-daily walks to the post office when he collapsed on the steps and was taken to the hospital. Again Mother was summoned to come at once if she wanted to see him before he died. She quickly made arrangements for someone to take care of us children and got to El Campo within hours. She told me that she braced herself before she walked into her father's hospital room, afraid she was too late. Her dad sensed her presence somehow, and although nearly blind, he recognized her in the doorway. He managed a smile, and looking at her, he sang "Dixie." It was his goodbye to her, and a memory so sweet she always teared when she told it.

❦

During this time, I became Mom's social secretary. Sometimes she would dictate letters to people she wanted to thank—Rudy, her art teacher in Del Rio, merited the first letter—or to decline invitations to weddings and anniversary parties or to respond to flowers sent, letters received, and the like. After the first few weeks, she often told me in a general way what she wanted to say, and I would write it out for her approval. I had let two people know on my own what was happening with Mother: Linda, a cousin on my father's side who was living in Del Rio during my high school years and had made my entry there very easy, and Gernot, an exchange student from Austria who had lived with us when I was in the seventh grade and who had hosted my parents and later my sister and me when we took trips to Austria.

Linda had been raised by her grandmother, her mother having died when Linda was about two. I printed the email response she'd sent so Mom could read it. The allusion to a miracle brought one of the few big smiles to her face during the month of March: *Dixie Davenport is the most beautiful woman I have ever known. When I think of her, I think of crisp white blouses, tucked in, of course, so neatly to show off her perfect figure. I think of perfect posture, a wonderful smile, grace, and sensibility— and her hair. I was always wishing that I could be more like her, but knew that I never, never could even come close. And I remember her everlasting patience with me in high school when she would try to teach me how to do my Algebra problems! She never gave up on me, and when I would finally catch on, she would praise me as if I had accomplished a miracle (she probably thought it was a miracle!!) She is the mother that I always wished for and the one I always wanted to be to my children. I never was, but sometimes, when I tried really hard, I came close. Please put your arms around her and tell her that I love her.*

Gernot wrote a lovely letter also which I read to Mom. It told of his memories when he had stayed with us so many years before, and of how he loved and respected her. Mother was making her goodbyes, and those who loved her often responded with graciousness and love.

❦

My mother had two brothers: Ed, her older brother who was born thirteen months before her (and who had died in January), and Bill, younger by two years. Bill and his wife Gussie live in south Texas, only about fifteen miles north of El Campo. They had stayed in touch with Bubba regarding Mom's health, and were told in March that they should plan on coming fairly soon if they wanted to make sure they could have a real conversation. I talked to Donn, Bill's son, and he said that he and his wife planned to bring Bill and Gussie up to Dallas, probably for a short visit midafternoon, and then making another short visit the next morning before they left for the drive back.

This was one of the weekends when I had to leave Saturday evening. I'd told Mom Saturday morning that Bill and his family were coming, and that they would see her for the two short visits. It was very important to her that she look nice for the visit. I put some makeup and lipstick on her, and combed a wave back into her hair. We dressed her in her most attractive outfit. She was worried that she might have to go to the bathroom when they were there, wasting valuable time, so she tried to be rested and ready for visitors by two-thirty. We waited, and they did not come. Mom grew sleepy, but couldn't relax enough to fall asleep in her recliner. She tried to read a little to distract herself. Finally at five o'clock, I had to leave. I was disappointed that I'd missed them and a little annoyed that Mom had been kept waiting. I taped on the outside of her doorway some envelopes for Bill and Donn, enclosing some old newspaper clippings about family members that I'd found in Mom's archives that I thought they would like to have.

Dixie Lee told me later that Mom said she'd been disappointed with the visit when they finally did arrive. They seemed a bit awkward around her, and left after only a short visit. She consoled herself by looking forward to a private conversation with Bill the next morning. She was up early to make sure she had finished breakfast and was dressed before they returned. She waited until noon; they never showed. Later they told my sister that Mom had seemed so tired the evening before, they decided not to tire her out more by going back to see her on Sunday.

It seemed like an understandable mistake to me, but I nonetheless stayed annoyed for several days on Mom's behalf. Obviously, Donn had forgotten what he'd told me about the two-day visit, didn't know I'd told Mother what to expect, and of course had no idea that Mom waited all the next morning for them to return. I did understand—but there were so few things Mom had to look forward to, I hated for her to lose out on something that might have been.

My disappointment for her reminded me of how I felt about Dad the day we moved their furniture from Del Rio up to Dallas. My father was already in Dallas in the nursing unit, too sick to participate in the move. He knew what day to expect us. The movers came much earlier than arranged, so Mom and the rest of us didn't get by to see him in the morning as planned. We got furniture arranged in the cottage, boxes unpacked, books in the bookcases, and pictures on the wall by about four o'clock. I was pleased that the new place had some of the "old home" feel to it, and was looking forward to bringing my father over in a wheelchair to check out the place we hoped he would soon be able to move into.

Mom, Bubba, Kay, and I walked the one hundred yards over the little bridge and up a small hill to the nursing floor where Dad was staying. As we got off the elevator at his floor, we saw him right away. He was sitting in his wheelchair at a small table facing the elevators so he could see who got off, wearing a favorite blue shirt Mom had made and I had embroidered for him years before, playing solitaire. All traces of my fairly overbearing father were gone. He saw us, broke into a big smile, and said with absolutely no reproach, "Hi! I've been waiting for you all day!" The wistfulness in his voice and eyes touched me in ways he rarely did. To have disappointed him, when he had so little to look forward to, was very sad. If he had been angry—his old reaction—I would have known how to respond, but this new wistful-ness caught me offguard in its poignancy.

❦

I don't know when I began preparing myself for my mother's death. When I was six, I read *Little Lost Bobo*—a reader about a fawn whose mother disappeared. She did not respond no matter how much he called to her, so Bobo had to learn to make it on his own. The resolution incensed me: Bobo's mother, it turned out, had been hid-ing from him, following at a distance. How dare she put him through all that!

Shortly afterward, I read *Bambi*. When this fawn's mother disap-peared, I told myself she would show back up. But no, the end of the book came and she apparently had been "really" killed. It was my first understanding that mothers would not always be around. A few years later I read *Little Women*, and for some reason copied the goodbye poem Jo wrote to Beth. I think I was struggling to understand what death takes away and what you get to keep.

I started a doctoral program in psychology at the height of the death and dying movement stimulated by Kübler-Ross' work. I read the books—academic and biographical—took a class on the topic, attended workshops, eventually led workshops. I also did an inde-pendent study with one of my favorite professors to explore the issue of loss in more depth; later, I offered such opportunities to several of my own graduate students. My first professional article was on grief. The thesis was that the most unbearable part of grief resulted from what I called "illusions of control." If we can give up our narcissistic belief that we should be able to control life and death, I wrote, loss will feel less threatening to us.

During this time that I was immersed in the topic, I had a dream: My graduate mentor, Earl, was very ill and needed his students' per-mission to die. I awoke from the dream in tears, knowing that he needed for me to be able to say yes, but finding it impossible. The dream stayed vivid for me for several days, and I revisited the ending, trying to give my consent. Eventually, as I focused on the dream, something changed. I was back by Earl's bed; he was waiting for my answer. This time he was in pain, which continued to mount, until, finally, I knew that I could not allow him to suffer more simply because of my own selfish unwillingness to let him go. I said yes.

Not many things that I learned in graduate school helped me directly with Mother's dying, except, I think, this dream.

A week or two after Bill's visit, Mother wanted to talk one afternoon about the songs that her father had written. Edward Lee and his family had sung at funerals and weddings when he was growing up in North Carolina, and during the time he lived in Dallas we know he was in a men's choral group. She said a day rarely went by that he didn't whistle or sing. When he was in his seventies he turned his hand to composing songs. He wrote a Christmas hymn, a sentimental tear-jerker ("you'll be sorry then, when I am far away"), the spirituals, and then one more about wishing he could see his early homeplace before he died.

That afternoon when she and I were talking, I mentioned that this song about the old wooden spout in North Carolina was the one I remembered her singing most often when I was a child. She agreed, saying that it had never seemed especially sad to her, just nostalgic. She had found her father's old home on one of our trips east, and she knew where the wooden spout was: on the spring, right by the spring house where they had kept milk and butter to stay cool.

I sang the chorus, and she joined in with the alto. We made a pretty good duet that afternoon:

> *O, the old wooden spout,*
> *The moss-covered spout,*
> *One more drink of water,*
> *E're the spark of life goes out.*

Easter came in 1999 on April 4. I decided that what I wanted to do for an Easter present for Mom was to write down a sampling of my memories of her, as my cousin Dorothy had done for her parents. It seemed that each weekend, Mother had fifty percent less energy than the week before, and I was torn between writing something short that I knew she could "get," or writing something longer and more complete. I opted for the second choice, with many misgivings.

The memories came in a flood, many from early childhood, but also from my teenage and young adult years, and continuing up to the last autumn's trip in New England. Recalling them let me reach into the past and touch each memory into life again. For several days, I let my mind roam over the years and collect images and feelings, to be put to words as accurately and briefly as I could.

I gave Mom my list on Saturday afternoon before Easter. It was a good day for her, and she was able to read them all the way through, smiling as she remembered the events I mentioned. She thanked me, put them down to ask some questions about my health, and then re-read them. The next morning she was asleep when I got there, the memories were beside her bed in an envelope marked: KEEP!

Memories of Mom

Selections from an original list

• Singing as you did your housework in Dickinson—sometimes hymns or a song of your dad's, but more often "Shoo, Fly," "Mammy's Little Baby," or "Oh, What a Beautiful Morning."

• Taking me all the way into Houston to try to replace the beloved red tassled boots I'd outgrown.

• Calling us during a thunderstorm to look at the lightning.

• Reading *Poky Little Puppy* to me—over, and over and over!

• Walking back in the house with me after we saw Bubba and Dixie Lee off to school and consoling me by letting me lick the jelly spoon.

• Sewing a wonderful wardrobe of doll clothes for my Christmas present from Mrs. Santa.

• Helping me make cookies the Christmas I was eight and singing "It Came Upon a Midnight Clear" with me.

• Dressed up in your pink strapless formal and carnation corsage, going to a dance—and putting the carnations in a vase for me when you got home.

• Letting me play jacks under the livingroom windows and never worrying about the scratched varnish.

• Rocking me when I was crying from the mumps.

• Living your faith in such a way that when I heard the lyric "bringing in the sheaves" and mistook it for "bringing in the *sheets*," I could picture perfectly you and Jesus out in the backyard bringing in the laundry and talking things over.

• Driving me by the migrant workers' shacks one south Texas winter day to show me why we needed to donate our outgrown jackets so people who needed them more could stay warm.

• Studying every weekend at Nana's library table as you worked to finish your college degree.

• Taking on an impossible job at West Ward, touching your students with your mind and heart, and showing them that learning English could be fun.

• Telling my eighth grade English teacher, *without checking*, that you were sure the books I was reading were suitable for an eighth grader.

• Talking to inanimate objects such as cars, vacuum cleaners, food— as in, "Well, then, fall down and make everybody hate you!"

• Pretending you were asleep when our boyfriends crashed my slumber party and we danced in the street at 2 A.M.

• Working every algebra problem in the book on the Del Rio porch the first summer before you taught "modern math."

• Walking up the sidewalk to the High School the day after Dad's dismissal as High School principal made the headlines—with your shoulders back, your head up, and a smile on your face.

• Laughing with me when the divinity I made for a bake sale had to be eaten with a spoon, and suggesting we color it pink.

• Being infuriated instead of scared when you caught someone trying to break into our house one night.

• Writing me faithfully once a week for years and years.

• Always showing a quiet strength in times of crisis—from Dad's near fatal reaction to penicillin to my newly married panic about how to remedy an extra cup of milk I had just put in the cake batter.

• Laughing when I smushed the peanut butter/cracker on Wes's head.

• Serving as friend/surrogate parent to all the Presbyterian ministers in Del Rio.

• Making me a nightgown with the crocheted yoke your grandmother had made for your mother.

• Visiting sick students and telling me you wished you'd kissed Bubba Dodson the last time you saw him before he died.

• Spending days before numerous Christmases in the kitchen baking with me in preparation for the family gathering—talking, laughing, catching up with each other, licking the beaters.

• Getting excited about finding one more elusive piece to the genealogy puzzle.

• Telling me your dream about using up your quota of patience with a difficult colleague and putting her headfirst in the garbage can!

• Taking painting classes after retirement and glorying in the colors and landscapes you could produce.

• Winning second prize in the state with one of those paintings.

• Never once complaining about all the medical procedures and surgeries of the last ten years.

• Working so hard with grace and courage to regain your strength after each medical setback, and quoting Nana—"Keep on keeping on."

• Sharing travels with me—New Jersey in '94, Britain in '95, Seattle in '96, Santa Fe in '97, and New England in '98—and doubling my pleasure because you were there, too.

• Showing my friend when you were eighty-four how you did your floor exercises and being a little disappointed at your difficulty in touching your toes to the floor behind your head.

• Taking a Creative Writing course at age eighty-seven and having your instructor urge you to write for publication.

• Showing graciousness toward everyone, regardless of their station in life.

• Looking at me with frank astonishment when I suggested that you could quit working on the checking balance, that it was "close enough."

• Passing on the Correll understanding of integrity, through your own example as well as by sharing stories like your dad's defying the KKK.

• Looking a nursing home administrator in the eye when he tried his "can-you-ever-forgive-me" manipulation, and telling him, "I can probably forgive you, but I will *never* condone what you've done."

• Always, always being there for us, loving us and showing us how to live with courage, grace, and joy.

I love you, Mom. I am so *blessed* to have you for my mother!

Day-to-day problems continued to happen very fast. By the time we figured out there was a problem and addressed it, something new and worse had occurred, and it was impossible to keep up, much less get ahead. In the previous years, we'd had more time. When Mom couldn't walk up to the Dining Hall, we'd gotten her a three-wheel scooter. If spinal stenosis caused excruciating pain, we found an anesthesiologist who could provide injections of cortisone and anesthesia that provided marked relief. When she became unable to sleep flat, we'd gotten her a hospital bed. There were always new things Mom wanted to learn, books she wanted to read, people and places she wanted to visit; all we had had to do was clear the barriers out of the way and her own zest and vitality flourished. I'd thought of her as the person I knew who was least susceptible to depression.

Although she was not depressed, the downhill slide was unmistakable. I thought back to February, when, still in her cottage, there had been times she could get out of bed and get back and forth to the bathroom without assistance. Now, back on the nursing unit, she always needed help getting in and out of bed, and overworked aides did not always respond promptly. She was on oxygen all the time. Within a few more weeks, she lost bladder control and they inserted a catheter, which lasted three days until she got a urinary tract infection. The decision was made by the staff to require diapers, a humiliation Mom tried not to dwell on. She did her best to accept these changes gracefully, as she had accepted other previous limitations, but she hated this assault to her dignity. I hated it for her, grieving that my mother should be reduced to spending her dwindling energy on such preoccupations.

The doctor was saying she could die at any time. They guessed that, given the rate she was losing ground, she probably had only weeks to live.

Perhaps, Bubba and Dixie Lee and I thought, hospice could help her return to her own cottage. We would get round-the-clock assistants who would not be too busy to attend to her. My brother called, and a hospice representative made plans to come out and finalize arrangements. This was the first possibility of our significantly impacting the quality of Mom's life, and we allowed ourselves to feel tentatively hopeful. The outcome of the attempt was at once frustrating, disappointing, and, paradoxically, pleasing.

That night my brother called to tell me what had happened. Prior to the scheduled meeting with hospice, the nursing home social worker met with Mom to explain that hospice was available to help her with the final months of her life. This was not the best beginning, as it turned out. Offended that someone would try to predict the time of her death—as if her own will were inconsequential—Mother would listen no more. The social worker was dismissed from the room, not allowed even to leave any brochures. Mother obviously had no intention of throwing in the towel at this point. Her refusal was not as gracious as her usual style, but still, a glimpse of some of the old clarity!

I had a try at it the next day when I was in Dallas. After catching up with each other for a few minutes, I began,

"You know, Mom, if you went with hospice, you wouldn't have to agree to die in six months. What do they know? You could fool them all, live as long as you want to, and in the meantime, be in your own cottage. What can they do to you anyway if you break their rule?"

"Honey, it's only for six months," she answered. "They won't let you use their services unless you are going to die in six months."

"Well, you're right—some doctor has to say that's your life expectancy. But how often are the doctors wrong? Remember the doctor that nearly killed you when you had ulcers and he told you to make yourself eat, that you were depressed and anorexic? And remember how they kept telling my student she had only a few weeks—months at the outside—to live? Twelve years later she's married, has three kids, and a fulltime job. Doctors are wrong all the time. We can make this one of those times to add to the list. Teaches them humility. It's good for them."

Mother smiled and looked tempted but unconvinced.

"I don't think so. There are too many arrangements to make. It's just too much trouble."

"We'll do it all, Mom. We can get someone to be with you around the clock. Let us kids take care of that. Don't you want to be back in your own place?"

"No, sweetie, I think I'll just stay here and let Dot [the floor's charge nurse] take care of me." She used her tone of voice that meant the discussion was over.

Shortly after the failed hospice incident, Mom was moved from a semi-private to a private room on the same floor. It was a small room, equipped with a hospital bed, a chest of drawers, and a couple of folding chairs. It was clean and serviceable, but hardly welcoming. Both my brother and I suggested that we bring over some of her furniture and pictures, but Mom declined. Too much bother, she said again. Peggy simply did it without asking. We had already had the recliner moved, and Peggy added a lamp table and lamp, several pictures of the immediate family, and Mother's painting of "Home." Peggy's reasoning was that if Mom didn't like them there, they could always be moved back over to the cottage.

Bubba and I mused about it later. Neither of us really understood why Mother would object to having her things there. I speculated that maybe it was easier for her just to make a clean break. Or perhaps, because thinking through the arrangements was now too hard for her, she thought that it would be too much trouble for anyone. We smiled at Peggy's quiet defiance. Bubba said, "When I asked Mom twice and she said no twice, I quit asking. I'm still her son! Good thing Peggy didn't have all those years you and I did growing up with her!"

It turned out that Mom was pleased with the additions, especially the painting that Peggy had hung right beside her bed. She told Peggy that when she woke in the night a little disoriented, she could look at the painting and know again where she was.

We decided to keep the cottage indefinitely. It was expensive, but keeping it gave Dixie Lee and me a place to stay when we came up, and we had access to Mother's files, clothes, and the like that we might want to find quickly. Besides, none of us was ready to divide things up and empty the cottage. We held onto a diminishing hope that somehow Mom might be able to return there to live, or more likely, to die.

Several years ago one of my friends' father died. Gary had been close to his father, and seemed to have the same mix of feelings that my mom evoked from me: admiration, love, appreciation. I heard from his wife that what comforted Gary the most in his profound grief was a dream he had about his father. As I remember, the dream flowed back and forth across his father's timeline—images of his father as a military officer, as an old man, as a young boy, a newly married husband, an adolescent—years when Gary knew his father as well as the years before Gary was born. The dream seemed to have allowed my friend to wrap his mind around the totality of who his father was, unconstrained by chronology or specific memories. Somehow, it helped.

I remember thinking, when I heard about the dream, that it fit with my understanding of the unconscious. Chronological time seems to be the conscious mind's arena; in dreams and imagery, we easily picture our grown children as toddlers, time can slow down or race, we can shift locations in the wink of an eye. As Freud said, "The unconscious, at all events, knows no time limit." I began to speculate that the unconscious mind is the older and perhaps wiser. Are we not closer to the reality of another person when we can allow all of the selves across a lifetime to comprise the person? It's a similar concept, I thought, to the idea of karma: that each person has an essence or a soul that is maintained against all odds.

I liked the idea of this. It provided a tentative, if fanciful, answer to one of my childhood worries: If there is a heaven, I used to wonder, where people can reunite with friends and relatives who predeceased them, how will Mother's cousin Gus ever recognize his dad, who died before Gus was born? How will his mom find him, since Aunt Jennie died when Gus was four and she was thirty, and the son she will be looking for died in his sixties? How can the mother/son relationship play out with the son twice as old as the mother? Now I could entertain the idea that if Gus and Jenny each had a reality that transcended specific ages and roles, they wouldn't need to recognize each other by physical clues in order to *know* each other. As with dreams, where the dreamer might later explain, "Well, I just knew it was Larry, even though it didn't look like him," the unconscious might have powers of discernment which would allow recognition.

By this time it was beginning to dawn on me that helping Mom die was not going to be hard in just one way. Some of the books I'd read described the task pretty simply, as if it were something that would be manageable with enough forethought and wisdom. So far, I counted, it had been hard learning to talk matter-of-factly with Mom about her dying. That had required an acceptance on my part that was heart-wrenching. Then it was hard seeing her lose ground so steadily, no matter how hard she tried what had worked before. Now it was hard because the ways that used to bring her some happiness were not working anymore. *How many more ways can there be for it to be hard?* I wondered. Depressed at that thought, I brooded for awhile. I took a walk and looked for rocks to kick. *You'll just have to be more creative,* I finally told myself. *Pay attention to what she can do, not what she can't, and go from there.*

So, late in April, my brother and his wife Kay and I tried something else that we thought might be a little fun for her. She had not been hungry in weeks, had forced herself to eat, but one Friday she told my brother that she thought Swiss steak would taste good. The three of us made plans: I would cook the steak, rice, gravy, and make a cake; they would drive down from north Dallas and bring the salad, dishes, napkins, flatware. We would take it all to Mom's room for Sunday lunch and have a meal with her there, all of us together, like old times. We got permission from the charge nurse.

Saturday Mother was feeling pretty good. She was alert, not in pain, not too exhausted. We talked off and on until early evening, when I left to begin cooking. I got back over there about nine o'clock Sunday morning, and found Mom sitting in the recliner, head down, dozing. I woke her up and her eyes looked glazed. "What's wrong, Mom? Can you tell me what's wrong?" Nothing. "Mom, wake up enough to tell me what's wrong. Do you need something?"

"I . . . need . . . . ." She couldn't finish the sentence.

"Can you tell me what you need? Tell me and I'll try to get it. What's wrong?"

"I . . . I . . . need . . . ."

She seemed hot. I got the nurse to take her temperature and vital signs: temperature of ninety-nine, she said, low blood pressure, rapid heartbeat. I waited awhile, touched her forehead again. She seemed hotter. Increasingly alarmed but unable to motivate the staff to pay much attention, I went over to the cottage to get a thermometer I was more sure of. 101.2 this time. Damn. Another infection. This was number three in the two months she'd been there. I got the nurse to call the doctor to authorize blood work and was that told blood would be drawn the next day. *Why not today so it can be sent to the lab earlier?* I argued, and got them to do it then. I called Bubba and Kay to let them know what was happening. They came, bringing the salad, but it was clear this was not going to be the family meal we had counted on.

The three of us ate at the cottage, searching for conversation topics that were far away from the obvious.

🌺

One Christmas in Del Rio during the 1980s, Mother and I were in the kitchen talking and cooking. Somehow the topic of reincarnation came up and she wondered why anyone would believe such a concept. I told her that I didn't think reincarnation was very likely either, although it did explain the powerful sense we sometimes have that we've known someone or been someplace before.

What worried me, I said, was one usual component part of the concept: that as we moved toward perfection in our cumulative lives, we "contracted" ahead of time to work on a specific difficulty by having the next life present us inescapably with situations which we would have to come to terms with.

Mother was listening. "For example, I hate being in a position when I have to depend on others for essentials," I continued. "Sometimes I worry that I agreed awhile back to have some lingering illness that will mean that I have to get more comfortable with dependency."

I paused and pondered that thought for a minute.

"I hope, if I did agree to that in a weak moment, that whoever I contracted with knows I'm a very fast learner. Very, very fast! A few days will be fine—I won't need months! In fact, I can learn an awful lot by reading a book!"

Mother nodded and we laughed about her being a fast learner too. "It's what I dread most," she admitted, "having a long final illness. I don't mind the dying, it's giving up my independence I would hate."

One of the things I always did in the nursing home was to stay in the room when the aides were tending Mother. One or two of them would come in, and with clear ideas of dismissing me, would say, "We're going to bathe your mother now."

I would smile and say, "Good! Here, let me back up a little and get out of your way."

Occasionally one of them would try again, "If you don't mind waiting outside. . ."

"Oh," I would answer brightly, "I always stay. Go right ahead. And the family wants to thank you for taking such good care of her!"

I had helped Mother during her previous hospital stays with all kinds of hygenic details, so her modesty had learned to accommodate my presence. Besides, I had no intention of missing out on seeing firsthand how they treated her, since by this point she was not in a position to remember and tell us if there were problems. Most of the aides were courteous and respectful, if not especially creative.

One of them, however, whose cute, bubbly approach at first misled me, only went through the motions. When she rolled Mom to her right side to bathe her and Mom groaned, I mentioned that it would hurt her a lot less if she were turned to her left side.

"But I'd have to move the bed. It's up against the wall!"

"Yes," I agreed. "It should take you about three seconds longer, six seconds if you count moving the bed back. It would mean a lot to her."

I showed her how easy it was.

Two weeks later I was there when the same aide again rolled her to her right side to bathe her. Mom was visibly trembling with pain and the effort to hold herself on that side.

"How about rolling her on her *left* side like we talked about before?" I asked.

The aide looked at me blankly. *Oh. Maybe she's not good on the difference between left and right.*

"Turn her so she's facing the door," I suggested.

The aide nodded, but then continued to hesitate. She frowned.

"*Now*," I said, in the authoritative tone I had instantly obeyed as a child when Mother used it. It still worked.

But, of course, I was not always there to insist.

❦

After preparing ourselves for the worst in March and April, we were relieved when Mother seemed to stay on a plateau during May and June. She was infection-free for those weeks, and had settled into a routine which felt okay to her. They had cut back on her Prednisone, and accordingly her vision had improved enough for her to read. My brother, sister, and I would bring back books from the cottage we thought she might enjoy re-reading, or find some large-print books in the nursing home library. She was usually strong enough to feed herself.

It was good to be able to catch our breaths for a bit and not worry so intensely about her condition. I was not much better at figuring out new things that might make her life more enjoyable, however. Once I suggested our getting her in the wheelchair and getting out for awhile—Spring was beautiful, the crepe myrtles were in bloom all over the grounds—and I thought she might enjoy going to spend awhile in the cottage, as she had during previous illnesses. No, she said apologetically. She was just too tired. I took over a tape recorder with the tape of Uncle Ed's family around the piano, but she couldn't pay attention. Another time I prepared some strawberry shortcake— a favorite of hers when she was well—but other than taking a few polite bites to please me, she was uninterested in eating. Her mood stayed, I told a friend, between 4.5 and 5.5 on a 10-point scale. Not sad, not angry, not depressed, but also not enthusiastic or joyful.

During the week, I would store up things to talk about with her. Little things: A wren had built a nest in my hanging bougainvillea and there was a baby bird in it. A cousin was engaged. A niece had a new boyfriend. I asked her to tell me more stories about Aunt Cord, asked what Easters had been like when she was a little girl, got her to look through catalogs with me to hunt for a suit I needed for a conference. I brought in lilies blooming for the first time at the cottage, the bulbs having been moved several years before from the site of her grandmother's house. To please me, I think, she tried to respond, but it was clear her heart was not in it.

She was, however, not getting worse. The internal hum I had gotten so accustomed to quietened a little. My sister and I agreed that we would alternate weekends in Dallas as long as Mother could maintain the plateau. If Mom needed me, I would be there, but if she didn't, I could use a break from the routine of working all week and spending every weekend in Dallas.

My first free weekend I stayed at home, doing nothing but catching up on my sleep, drinking diet Dr. Peppers, talking on the phone, and reading murder mysteries. Ah, the luxury of laziness! I had two hot fudge sundaes in place of meals, and added decadence to laziness as the bases of a possible lifestyle change.

The other free weekend I had before Mom's condition worsened again, I went to stay with some friends in Austin, Carole Ann and her husband, Pat. Carole Ann had mentioned on the phone that Mary Chapin Carpenter was having an outdoor concert that weekend about fifteen miles west of Austin. As an early birthday present for me, she got us tickets. That weekend at Carole Ann and Pat's was delightful. I swam in their pool. I ate the delicious food Pat prepared. I let myself be taken care of.

And we went to the Carpenter concert.

I hadn't been to an outdoor concert in years. It had been rainy that day, but by evening a breeze came up and blew off the clouds. Most of the humidity was gone and the night lacked the usual Texas June heat. As Carole Ann and I waited for the concert to begin, we settled back: commented on audience members, got something to drink, enjoyed catching up with each other. We had been friends since graduate school days, so it was great just hanging out with her.

Then Carpenter came on stage, blonde hair blowing in the breeze, enjoying the hospitality of Texas, wanting to sing. I found that I could not sit still—too much rhythm and pent-up energy. I did not embarrass Carole by getting up to dance in the aisle, but I did sing along and let my feet dance. Then came the song I'd heard on the radio recently, entitled "I'm Almost Home." I wasn't sure of the lyrics of the chorus. When I heard them clearly, I mentally filed them away under "Home" with the other songs that seemed to have increasing importance to me:

> *I'm not running*
> *I'm not hiding*
> *I'm not reaching*
> *I'm just resting in the arms of the great wide open*
> *Gonna pull my soul in*
> *And I'm almost home*

This became one of the songs I later found myself humming at night when I walked my dog. There was something about the combination of letting go and security that I needed to understand in relation to Mother, but I couldn't quite get it. So I sang the chorus to myself and waited to see if clarity would come.

❦

During this relatively worry-free period there was nothing hard for me to learn in order to be with Mom. By now I understood that more hard times would surely come, but for awhile I could relax and play a little.

Gradually some of Mom's energy returned, and we again could sometimes have conversations that lasted more than a few minutes. I took some of her old photo albums over for us to talk about, photos of her from about ages eleven to twenty-five. In her room also at this time were portraits of her made during these early years that we had chosen to have reproduced for family members. I had known that the El Campo photographer thought she was the prettiest girl in town and had frequently taken her picture free so that he could use it for advertising display. Now, in going through them, Mother mentioned casually that when she was at the University of Texas., an Austin photographer asked for the same arrangement—hence the large number of portraits at a time when most people couldn't afford to have even one made.

As she always had, Mother dismissed any remarks about her beauty. It was amazing to me that as much data as she had to the contrary, she had never thought of herself as pretty, or if she did, it just wasn't something that mattered very much.

Looking at one black and white picture of her when she was about sixteen, I asked if she remembered what color the dress was that she wore. She did indeed. It was a brown plaid, with black lace on the collar and cuffs and a six-inch-wide black leather belt. That little blob of white under the belt was the handkerchief she had taken to school that hot day, tucked under the belt so she wouldn't have to carry a purse. I asked about another: Ivory organdy with a pink ribbon sash. Her eyes lit up as she went back in time and touched the colors again with her mind. *Ah, this was fun for her!* For a couple of hours we looked at pictures and she described the dresses, most of which she had made, and the bright colors she had chosen. She grew more animated as we talked about high school and college days: happy, active times for her in spite of having very little money. I discovered a snapshot of her taken at this time: Mom at nineteen, grinning with delight at being in her first snowfall.

As she talked, I listened as I do with my patients, envisioning her at an earlier time in life, resonating to the feelings and attitudes that made up her inner world and helped shape who she was to become. In a way that I hadn't before, I got to know the young Dixie. She was so easy to like! So much enthusiasm, an ability to carry responsibilities easily, a sunny outlook even during dark times. The strength and warmth that I had seen in her since I had been a child I could now trace to the younger Dixie. The light that had been unquenchable until this last January shone in recognizable fashion in her face through all the years. It gave some perspective to this last dreadful year, almost as if 1999 didn't count in the big scheme of things. This year was not about *her*, it was about what was happening *to* her.

❦

Five or six years ago I participated in a hypnotherapy workshop. The leader of the workshop was Earl, my mentor from graduate school, about whom I had had the dream years before. He had continued offering training workshops after his retirement from teaching. The usual understanding among mental health professionals is that the best way to learn a therapeutic technique is to volunteer in a demonstration and thus experience the technique as the receiver. Accordingly, when Earl indicated a willingness to demonstrate an age regression technique called Affect Bridge, I volunteered.

The entire process was too complicated to describe in detail. The heart of it, however, was that I went back in time to being a toddler. I was alone in my crib, very scared, and crying for Mother, who did not come. Finally I fell back asleep. As the scene moved into the next morning, Mother came in to get me. I tried to tell her how scared I'd been and she picked me up to comfort me. As I progressed through the day, my sense was that every time Mom started to put me down, I panicked and clutched her tighter, so she went through her housework holding me on her hip with one arm until I was all right again.

The scene was very vivid and quite powerful. I have no idea in retrospect whether the incident ever happened. I rather think it did not, although it is possible that having put us kids to bed, my parents took a thirty-minute walk or something of that order, so might not have been there to hear me call. My hunch as I look back on the experience, though, is that I had projected the present childlike part of myself onto the baby in the scene; the fear, then, would likely represent current worry that when Mom died, I would feel the terror of abandonment.

Although the complete scene from start to finish was comforting, it did leave me with lingering concerns about some possible lurking dependency in my unconscious. Could I, in fact, handle Mother's death when it came? How much of me did the baby in the scene represent?

❦

During June, Mother and I again discussed what she wanted as funeral arrangements. Her main requirement was that the service not be "doleful." She had never been doleful, didn't like dolefulness, and would have none of it at her funeral. Grandchildren, if they wished, would be allowed to offer some brief memories of her, as long as they were not doleful.

At this point, I raised my eyebrows and smiled, "Wait. Let me see if I have this straight. You don't want anything doleful, right?"

She answered, "That's right. I won't have doleful."

"Okay," I responded. "I think I get it. What songs do you want?"

"Let's see. I have to have 'How Firm a Foundation' sung to the tune of *Adeste Fideles*. It's not in the blue hymnbook; you'll have to copy it from the red one. That's the song, you know, that my grandmother [Edward M.'s wife] always sang when she finished praying for my grandfather who was off fighting in the Civil War. Seeing her get up from her knees and begin singing that song was one of my father's earliest memories of her.

"Then I want 'How Great Thou Art' Another one I like is 'Mighty God, While Angels Bless Thee.' Maybe that should be the first one. Also, see if you can get a soloist to sing 'Swing Low, Sweet Chariot.' They sang it for my dad, and it was just beautiful.

"And I want that song with the trumpet herald. "God of Our Fathers." That should be the recessional. I've already asked Sarah Cramer to play that and she agreed. She promised to really bang it out! I want to exit on a note of triumph. The whole service should be triumphant."

"You don't want anything doleful?" I asked, trying to sound perplexed. This was a game we knew how to play.

She gave me one of her looks, half amused, half stern.

I showed her a bulletin from a funeral service that I had found in the family files. I liked the beautiful colored picture on the front and the scripture underneath. Did she want this as the funeral bulletin? Yes, she did. I showed her a poem she had saved and marked "beautiful." Did she want that on the back cover of the bulletin? Yes, that would be fine.

"I've told Sandy [her minister] that I would like him to mention in the sermon that my great-uncle Will Lowrance was the founding pastor of the church here, and that being able to be a member of this church made my move to Dallas sort of like coming home."

Again the subject of attire came up. At Thanksgiving when we had discussed it, she had decided on a white dress. Having thought about it some more, she told me now that she'd decided she wanted more color. She couldn't go with the red that she knew I would like, but she did agree on a mint green suit I had bought her a couple of years before. "With some color close to the face: a pretty scarf or necklace or corsage." She looked at me. *"Pink*, not red."

She thought for another minute. "I don't want to be buried flat-chested. I don't know how they do it, but if a bra isn't enough, have them poof me up somehow."

"Poof?"

"You know what I mean." Stern look.

"Yes, I do, absolutely. I'll make sure you're poofed." Mother had never said a word about it, but I knew she was proud that she had kept her beautiful figure all these years. *Of course* I could understand why she wanted to look her best as she went into eternity.

We talked a little about caskets and what she wanted at the cemetery service. The mood, amazingly, continued in the same light-hearted vein.

"Okay, pallbearers. Everard [my brother's real name] and John [Dixie Lee's husband] first. Then the grandsons Wes and Lee, with Doug and Tim [her grandsons-in-law] last. Oh, and I want the estate to pay for a babysitter for Alyssa [great-granddaughter] so she won't get restless sitting so long."

"Gee, Mom," I teased, "anything else? Do you want to specify the weather?"

"Cool would be good. Sunny but cool."

Funeral plans having been completed in this pleasant fashion, Mom and I talked awhile about death's being a natural end to life, something that occasionally even offered some humor. I reminded her of an event she had written me about that had taken place about ten years before.

My father's older cousin, Leah, also lived in Del Rio. During her last months there she required constant care, and at the slightest emergency, caregivers called Mom to tell them what to do. Mom made numerous trips over to Leah's apartment to assess the situation and advise them on proper procedures.

One afternoon they called again and said that Leah was dying, could Mom come at once? Of course. She dropped what she was doing and rushed over. Leah was quite pale, breathing shallowly, and unresponsive to questions. She seemed restless and from time to time, called out a name.

"Who's 'Gayle'?" one of the caregivers asked.

"Oh, my, that's her daughter," Mom responded. "She died of polio in her early twenties and it nearly broke Leah's heart."

As Leah continued whispering Gayle's name, the caregivers agreed that she must be in another realm of consciousness, able to see her daughter but not quite able to reach her. A sense of awe at what was apparently taking place settled over the bedroom.

Leah's voice grew more urgent. "Gayle! Gayle!," she called. Her arms raised a little. "Gayle!" It was a demand now.

Mom spoke quietly to her, telling her she was going to be all right, that Gayle was waiting for her.

Hearing Mom's voice, Leah roused a little. She shook her head, frowned heavily, and opened her eyes. Then she glared at my mother.

"Dixie!" she said quite crossly. "What are *you* doing here?!"

❧

That night I remembered that Mom was not the first in her family to plan her funeral so carefully. My Aunt Cord had also been specific about her wishes regarding procedures that were to follow her death. Years before she died, she made herself a blue dress—very simple, small print, buttoned down the front—and announced that this was the dress she was to be buried in. There was to be no adornment and certainly no lipstick. Not one to condone waste of any sort, she wore that dress to church nearly every Sunday in the years before she died.

Aunt Cord also specified that she wanted no man to touch her body, even after she was dead. The *wife* of the local mortician was to lay her out. This last directive elicited her sister Em's scorn, but Em nonetheless made sure Cord's wishes were followed.

❧

The last weekend in June I told Mother about a recurring dream I was having.

"I've been dreaming that you can walk again. You're using a walker, but you can *walk*! You know they've cut your Prednisone dosage to ten mg a day, so maybe you can get stronger now that you don't have that holding you back."

Mother shook her head but smiled wistfully. "Wouldn't that be nice, honey?"

I had to leave midafternoon that Saturday. The next day I got a call from Bubba. It seemed that Saturday night as the aides were helping her get ready for bed, she said she wanted to see if she could take a step. With their supporting a good deal of her weight, she did manage one step, the first one in months.

Sunday she took two steps, Monday three.

I called Bubba at work on Wednesday to see if the trend had continued. He said that Mom had told him at lunch that she'd wanted to try again the night before, but the night nurse said she couldn't walk without the doctor's permission. She'd also been wanting physical therapy and she wanted out of diapers during the day time. Seems the doctor would have to give permission for those things also.

This did not sit well with my brother. As he related it, he went to the charge nurse, explained that this approach was bullshit, that

Mother was to be allowed to do what she felt strong enough to undertake. He tracked down the physical therapists and told them the same thing. Effective that day, changes were made. Having a son who could slip easily into his masterful attorney mode had many benefits for Mother.

❦

At about this time, Mom's vision, which had cleared up a bit, again began blurring. I asked Dot, the charge nurse, to locate an optometrist in the Dallas area who had a mobile unit, one that could come out to the nursing home and test Mom's vision to see if a new prescription might be able to help her read small print again. We had found that bookstores and libraries offered very limited selections of larger print books, and tape-recorded books were out of the question because of Mother's hearing loss; new glasses might be a real benefit. Dot found what we needed, and an appointment was scheduled for a week or so later.

One week after Mom began trying to walk, I got a call from Dixie Lee, who was in Dallas for a few days. She said that Mother was much worse, in bed all the time, feeling sick, and throwing up. The next day the report was even more alarming: Mom had had diarrhea all night in addition to continued vomiting. She was miserable. By now I had learned that trying to talk with the doctor in charge of her case was impossible. The man was never available and he never returned phone calls. I was beginning to categorize him with unicorns—a mythical beast. I called the nurse practitioner, who at first sounded fairly knowledgeable. Mother's blood work indicated that she was pre-leukemic, she told me, but they were not recommending further diagnostic tests or treatment.

What was causing the intestinal problems? They weren't sure. I told her that if Mother couldn't take liquids, she would get dehydrated very fast, and asked that they please start IV's. Could they do that?

"Well," Debbie hesitated, "but insurance won't pay for that unless she's in the hospital."

"Don't worry about insurance. We'll pay for it. Just don't let her get dehydrated or she'll get much worse very quickly. We don't want her to have to make another trip to the hospital. You all *can* do IV's, right?"

"M-m-m," said Debbie noncommittally.

The next day my sister called to say that Debbie had told her that an x-ray had indicated an intestinal blockage of some sort—an ileus—and they had switched Mom to a liquid diet.

"I thought she couldn't keep liquids down," I said.

"Yes, that's right."

"So they are switching her to a liquid diet, knowing it won't work? What are they thinking?"

Dixie Lee didn't know.

"Have they started IV's?"

"No, not yet."

I took a deep breath and told myself to calm down. I've never been very good at waiting through incompetence, and I was increasingly convinced that that was what was happening with Mom. I struggled for an alternative to calling up Debbie and yelling at her. *This is my mother! How dare you take such a casual attitude when she is so sick?!* The only alternative I could think of was to get formal medical information that might carry more weight with Debbie than my worry had.

I went to the medical school library at A&M and spent a few hours looking through references to see what the consensus was on "ileus." I bought one of the recommended references for the lay public. What I found was that it was a very serious condition and needed to be treated immediately. No food or liquid at all until the intestinal pressure could be reduced. Until then, the patient was to be on IV's.

I called my sister back and told her what I'd found. By now I was both angry and frantic, convinced that the nurse practitioner was mishandling Mother's treatment. Dixie Lee said the staff wanted to wait and see if the liquid diet would help. This made no sense to me and my agitation doubled. Desperate by now, I called my brother to solicit his help; he also felt, like my sister, that we should trust the nursing staff. What occurred was one of our few disagreements: I thought that the staff didn't know appropriate treatment, and I suspected they also did not know how to start IV's. I wanted Mother's gastroenterologist to be called in for consultation. My brother and sister disagreed. This was the first time we could not function as a team.

On Thursday, I got a call that Mom was on her way to the hospital. Four days after the problem began, the nurse practitioner finally decided that maybe Mother was getting dehydrated, and she attempted, unsuccessfully, to start an IV. It seemed that Mom was by this time too dehydrated to find a vein that could take the IV needle. They had called an ambulance.

I said I was coming up.

I found when I got there that the medical technician in the ambulance had been successful in getting the IV going; Mom was in a hospital room, her gastroenterologist had been called and would be in shortly. Her internist was also coming by. They had her on oxygen and had given her blood, trying to get the white count down. She was lethargic, but not in pain. We talked a little, I cut her fingernails for her, and she dozed.

The gastroenterologist finally examined her and eventually determined that there was no indication of ileus. We never found out what happened to it, or if the diagnosis was in error. The internist said that Mom's intestinal problems were the result of being over-medicated; he cut out some medications and cut down on others. Mother was anxious to get out of the hospital, so with nothing else to do that might help, in a few days she was transported back to the nursing unit. In retrospect, the only good thing that came out of this hospital trip was that she got to see two of her previous doctors, both of whom she liked immensely.

By now it was early July. After this dehydration episode, Mother became progressively weaker; she was to spend her last two months in bed, too weak and exhausted to sit up or to try to read, and often unable to feed herself. We canceled the appointment with the optometrist.

This episode marked the beginning of my certainty that whatever was wrong with Mom was beyond the ability of nurses and doctors to treat effectively, even on a short-term basis. She quickly became dehydrated again; her electrolytes continued to move further and further from normative levels. Was she continuing to have small storkes? What symptoms might be attributable to her incredibly high white count? Since she didn't get any stronger after she left the hospital, had the internist's diagnosis of overmedication been incorrect? And what part did the long-term effects of Prednisone play?

Up until now, even if no one could fix it, I wanted to know what was wrong. In my mind, knowing the name of a problem seemed to offer the hope that it could perhaps be treated. Now, I told myself to quit asking. The answers that I got were often contradictory, and none of Mom's conditions seemed treatable anyway. It was very frustrating that no one knew how to help her, but what was especially enraging was the mantle of authority that medical personnel cloaked themselves in to avoid admitting inadequacy. I spent a satisfying moment visualizing my offering a required workshop in communication skills for all doctors, teaching them to say, "I don't know."

The downhill trend we had observed in Mom's condition during the Spring resumed, now on a steeper slope than before. As with my father when he was in his final decline, I began to limit what I would fight hard about to the issues of keeping her free from pain and from being afraid. Again, my siblings and I felt that it would be a matter of weeks before she died, although the internist had said that he wouldn't be surprised if she survived six more months.

What should I hope for? I thought back to a seminar I had attended years before when a woman described what it was like watching her child die. She talked about hope. She said that she always had *some* hope, but that hope got increasingly narrow. At first she hoped her child would recover. Then she hoped Shari could live through high school, and then had to cut that back to hoping her daughter could live till her birthday. Eventually, her hope was that Shari's death would be peaceful and pain free. One of my thoughts when I heard this was that it sounded pretty dismal; what was the point of hoping at all?

Now I was beginning to understand that hope is not a willful decision, nor is deciding what to hope for very logical. I hoped for something until reality hit me so hard in the face with the impossibility of that hope that I was forced into a fallback position. I wasn't prepared yet to give up entirely, but the constant need to retreat to lesser positions was exhausting and depressing.

My somewhat cynical attitude about the competence of medical personnel actually began several years previously. The winter after my father died, Mom began having serious digestive problems—diahrrea, difficulty getting food down, and stomach cramps. On her first visit to her new family practice physician, he put her on a bland diet. Things got worse. On her second visit, he informed her that she was anorexic—due to depression over Dad's death, he told her with authority—and that since this was only psychological, she must make herself eat. Mom always followed doctors' orders, so she tried; she quickly became much sicker. Finally, after the third visit (two months after the problem began), the doctor checked her into a hospital for some tests. He explained to me parenthetically that Mother's memory about the sequence of symptoms could not be relied on, inasmuch as her brain, like a computer that wears out, just wasn't functioning very well any more. I showed him the daily diary she had kept, but he was unimpressed.

I told Mom about his brain/computer analogy. She raised her eyebrows and gave me a long look. Without much ado, she agreed to dismissing this doctor and transferring to a gastroenterologist as her primary physician.

This new doctor's endoscopic exam revealed a very serious case of ulcer disease. He could not see into the duodenum because by now it was completely blocked by ulcers. Treatment began and Mom slowly recovered, but it took months. If we had stayed with the initial physician, she would certainly have died.

In addition to added cynicism, however, this episode did bring one nice memory.

One weekend when I was visiting her in the nursing wing where she was recuperating, I brought in her tape recorder and a tape that she had received in the mail. Knowing that Mother was Presbyterian, friends of mine had made a cassette recording of many of the well-known Reformed hymns.

"Here's your mail, Mom. You got a package."

"Really? Who's it from?"

"Tom and Connie Hurlocker. It's a tape of traditional hymns that they recorded for you from a record. Want to hear it?"

Her face lit up.

"Oh, yes!"

"Now?"

"*Right* now!"

The tape recorder had no bass/treble control. The choral music was beautiful, but the pipe organ in the background made the words indistinct. I wished there were a way to turn up the treble. Mom listened to a song and then said,

"It's lovely, isn't it? I just have a little trouble hearing the words enough to recognize the song."

"Okay, I'll tell you the name of the song after the first line, so you'll know what to listen for."

That worked a little better, but not much. I thought about running back over to the cottage for one of her hymnbooks, but hated to interrupt the moment. These were songs I'd heard all my life and I knew most of the words.

I turned down the volume a little and began to sing for her over the music.

Mom smiled and closed her eyes. I sat by her bed and sang along with the tape for about twenty minutes, Mom listening intently. Every once in awhile she would nod in pleasure, and occasionally shake her head gently if I got a word wrong. She had missed going to church, and this made up for it.

The sweetness of those twenty minutes did not compensate for the unnecessary illness, but I did come away with a lovely memory.

❦

I was teaching a doctoral seminar during July. My brother called my home long distance almost every day around one o'clock to report how Mom had been during his daily lunch visit, and I called in for his message when I gave my class a break halfway through class. It was rarely good news. Each day on my way back to the seminar, I told myself that in the future I should wait until class was over before retrieving messages, but my need to be informed in an ongoing way usually won out. I wanted to know everything and at the same time I dreaded knowing. I told myself a little bitterly that this year was providing great opportunities for me to learn firsthand the psychological effects of ongoing failure and ambivalence.

The internal hum that had diminished in May and June now became an ongoing alarm, a frightening, discordant buzzing deep in my chest that was impossible for me to ignore. My reaction was the fight-or-flight adrenaline surge you get when you hear the rattle of a rattlesnake. With rattlesnakes the only wise approach is to run. But flight was not an option here, and, alas, there was no one to fight.

You, who took such care of yourself,
Who were such a good steward:
If the doctor said—walk two miles—
You walked three.
If he said—cut down on fats—
You counted every gram.
If she said—do these exercises every morning—
You did them first thing after rising. . .

You, who took such joy in color:
Who dressed always in splendid hues,
Who used paints so fearlessly,
Who gloried in sunsets and autumn leaves . . .

You, who merged joy and duty so effortlessly,
Who never spoke with bitterness,
Whose caring was so free, so easily given. . .

My mother, I will remember you so.
These were your graces, blessings you bestowed.

There is evil, I now know. I see it.
Destruction that attacks you,
That deprives you of choice,
That undermines your every effort.
It feeds on our despair.

My mother, it shall not win.
This battle is not the last.

So when you die,
When it has taken you away—
Piece by piece until finally gone—

I will remember your love, your colors,
The melody that is you.
In some shining part of me,
Your song will still be sung.

More: Nothing can touch what I prize the most.
Far past these indignities,
Past your death, past mine also,
Through all the eons yet to come,
I will always be your daughter.

🐝

I am not sure whether Mother's swearing took place the week before or after she was in the hospital.

She had had periods during the Spring when her internal thermostat quit working; she might have chills for no apparent reason for thirty minutes. Uncontrollable shaking, pallid skin tone, "freezing to death," as she said. Blankets, up to seven of them at once, did not help. On this occasion, however, the trouble was that she was hot. It did not help that the air conditioning had not worked in her room for a week. This, in the middle of a Texas summer!

Dixie Lee called that night. She told me about her efforts, in vain, to cool Mom down with a sponge bath, a fan directed on her, and a change to a lightweight cotton gown. Mother stayed hot and got increasingly agitated.

Dixie Lee described what happened. "She was crying and yelling and she *swore!*"

"Really? Mom swore?!"

"Yes!"

"What did she say?"

"She said 'I am *damned* hot!' And she said it more than once!"

I laughed out loud, thinking of the contrast between what Mother had said and what I would have likely said in her situation. I was pleased that she had recourse to uncharacteristic vocabulary when the situation demanded it.

I remembered telling Mom a story my cousin Edward had related to me about his mother, who, like Mom, never said even a "darn it." Edward was home from college for Easter vacation, and had been met at the bus by his sister. Dorothy warned him that Aunt Jimmie had put in and taken out a sleeve in Dorothy's Easter suit five times already, and was not in a good mood. When Edward got home, there was no Aunt Jimmie to meet him at the door with a big hug as she always had. Hearing the sewing machine going in another room, Edward tiptoed back in time to hear his mother say, "Oh, *damn* this damn material!"

In shock, he opened the door and peered in. "Mother??"

She looked up—still no welcome—and said, "Well, I think I'm doing well to limit myself to just *one word*."

Mom had laughed when I told her the story. I felt pretty sure that she was remembering Aunt Jimmie when she tried her own hand at profanity.

By focusing on the "swearing" part of Dixie Lee's message, I was able to keep my reactions to Mom's crying and yelling at more of a distance. None of us had ever heard our mother yell. I saw her cry only a couple of times. Even when she was very sick, if I asked how she was feeling, she would try to smile and say, "I think maybe I'm a little better." When the spinal stenosis was at its worst, before we found an anesthesiologist, she moved from a sitting to a standing position with so much pain that she would turn white and tremble, but she did not make a sound. The crying out in pain that began in July was understandable if I stayed objective, but otherwise it brought on new grief and anger. I hated, *hated*, this process that had the power to continue to reduce Mother's will and presence.

❦

There was something familiar about the feel of July, but at first I couldn't pinpoint what it was. I would go up to Dallas, spend time with Mom but often be unable to connect for more than a few minutes, and then come home. After awhile I realized that what I was recognizing was the sense of confusion and helplessness I'd felt in the Spring. I found that once again none of my internal or external ways of being in relation to Mom was working. It was hard again, in a whole new way.

In the Spring I had had the hope that it was possible to connect with Mother if only I were creative enough. Now, I understood there was nothing I could do. Day after day my brother called to say that Mom had slept through his lunch visit; if she was awake, she was often listless and uncommunicative.

It was exactly 173 miles from my house to the nursing home parking lot, whether I went through Waco or took the loop around it. If I left Bryan by midmorning, Friday, I could make it to Mom's room by lunchtime. By staying with her most of the time until I left midafternoon Sunday, I increased the odds of being with her in the random hour or two she might be more herself.

My cousin Edward called for an update and asked if Mom was "alert." I didn't know how to answer. The line between asleep and awake used to be clear to me; maybe "groggy" came in the middle. Now I saw that the continuum was between unconscious and being clearly herself, and that the area in between was messy and complicated. Was she alert if she could only answer questions in one-syllable words? Was she alert if she recognized me but her eyes stayed cloudy? Did it count if she seemed to understand something but later had no memory of it?

Eventually, the issue no longer interested me. If, at some point during my visit, she opened her eyes when I kissed her on the forehead, and kept them open for five minutes, I counted the visit a success. Sometimes when Bubba, Dixie Lee, or I were in the room, she would open her eyes slightly and let her gaze rest on our faces. I hoped she saw love. I learned to sit in a chair pulled up close to her bed so that if she did open her eyes, she could see me. If her eyes sparkled with some of the light I had taken for granted all my life, if I really got *her* back for a few minutes, it felt like a small miracle.

A minister friend of mine once told me his definition of miracle: a situation in which one senses the presence of God.

Mother's faith, I knew, was uncomplicated. It was not important for her to understand everything, because God was good and He loved her. She knew that He was taking care of her, no matter how the situation might appear objectively. Once when she was very ill, she told me that when she prayed, it felt as if she were a child, sitting on the floor with Jesus in a chair beside her, his hand resting on her head.

My psychological understanding of her image was that it captured her experience of her father. While I liked to think it also captured reality about God, I was not positive, but I was glad that Mom had an understanding that offered her such comfort, and I wanted to support her belief.

My own religious beliefs are less definable than hers. I use the word "God" to describe something more mysterious than her version of God. God, for me, is an essential mystical connectedness—a unity based on caring—and I know that moments of intense personal connection to nature or another person feel transcendent. If I use Ken's definition of miracle, then these small moments of renewed connection with Mom in July did indeed feel miraculous.

The awful destructiveness of the process at work on Mom's presence felt nothing like God. I was very angry at what was happening to Mom, but I did not hold God accountable. At one point, my brother, in despair at what was happening to Mom, said on the phone that it felt as if she were receiving the wrath of God, a consequence of some horrible sin. Understanding that he was speaking metaphorically, I responded in the same vein. It didn't feel to me that God was the source of the destruction; instead, it felt to me more that God was taking a nap, sleeping on the job. In this crisis, my theology regressed: God needed to wake up—*now, at once*—and put a stop to this nonsense.

In June of the previous summer, I had taken Mother to Virginia as a surprise for her brother Ed's eighty-ninth birthday. Charlie, Uncle Ed's youngest and also Mom's godson, is a talented guitarist and was there for the celebration. I believe he asked Mother about the songs her father had written. At any rate, she decided he needed to know, so when she returned to Dallas she copied her father's handwritten music and began writing what she knew of the history of each song. Unable to complete the task before she became too weak, she asked me to go back through the files and find her originals. I found the songs one evening among my grandfather's letters to his sister Cord and took them back over to her the next morning.

When I got there, she was asleep. I sat by her bed and looked them over, trying to imagine what my grandfather had been feeling when he wrote them. I began singing softly so as not to waken Mom, sightreading the melodies. One of them was a spiritual in memory of Hannah, Frank's wife. Hannah had cared for Edward Lee when his mother traveled to the Confederate Hospital in Richmond to nurse her wounded husband after the battle at Chancellorsville. As I sang this song to myself, Mother gently shook her head. I stopped in surprise and looked at her. "Sorry, you need more *swing*!" she said, and proceeded to sing the chorus for me:

> *Come along and let's go to heaven,*
> *Come along and let's go to heaven,*
> *Come along and let's go to heaven,*
> *My Lord, open the door today!*

Great! So I practiced until I got it right.

❦

I had grown up hearing my mother hum and sing. She sang as she went about her housework, she sang to us children when we needed comforting, and later, she sang in the Del Rio Presbyterian Church choir beside me. She did not have a trained voice, but her pleasant, light soprano provides the background music of many of my childhood memories.

Mom loved to talk about her dad's singing. As Postmaster, he was known by his coworkers to sing or whistle softly if he was working on a problem, a volume in contrast with his burst of music when he reached a solution. One of Mom's favorite stories took place on a Christmas Eve in the 1880s when Edward Lee was riding with the Texas Rangers at a small outpost in west Texas. The Rangers were bored, lonesome, and drunk, and by midnight, fights were beginning to break out. My grandfather brought out his guitar—carried around with him on horseback, I assume—and began singing Christmas carols. The men quietened and then began singing with him. Writing about the incident many years later in a newspaper column, my grandfather said he ended the impromptu concert by singing several nostalgic songs about home to remind the men of the families they had left. They slipped off to their bedrolls, one by one, many in tears, and the brawl was avoided.

As Mother aged, some of her enjoyment in singing diminished, and she sang only in church. After her move to Dallas when she was eighty-three, however, I noticed on several trips that she had a hymnbook propped up on the counter over the kitchen sink. I asked if she was practicing her singing again, and she answered, "No. I've decided I need to work on my whistling!"

❦

My niece Peggy and I both have birthdays at the end of July. Bubba and his wife Kay decided they should have a joint birthday party for us the night of July 23. A couple of days before the party, Bubba made his daily lunch visit to the nursing home. He found Mom not only awake, but able to converse with ease and spontaneity.

During my class break, I called home as usual to retrieve his message. I could hear it in his voice before he said the words: He felt terrible. He said that he'd been chatting with Mom about the upcoming birthday festivities to be at their house and that she had grown enthusiastic about the plans. Suddenly he realized that she had misunderstood. She thought he was inviting her to join us for the party. He had had to tell her she wasn't strong enough to make the trip up to north Dallas.

I was used to things being hard, but this was excruciating. For Mom to want something again—to get her hopes up and look forward to a family celebration—and then to have it snatched away, this was just too sad. I brushed the tears away that had come instantly, went back to finish class, and finally was able to go home. I felt bad for both of them: Bubba, for having to tell her no, and Mom, for being so disappointed. I felt bad for me, too. It felt especially hard that the party was partially for me, and, like Mom, I would have loved for her to be with me for one more birthday party. She had always made birthdays special for us: special cake, special presents, often a loving note or letter from her. We both knew this would be my last birthday with her still alive. To think of her feeling excluded from the family get-together broke my heart.

It took a long time to quit crying. Finally I pulled myself together, made myself some lemonade, and called Bubba at work. He was still feeling devastated at having to be the bearer of bad news. I told him I thought that we should have the party in Mom's room rather than his house.

Both of us knew this was a calculated risk. We had planned a Christmas night celebration for my father when he was in the hospital close to death, and it had failed miserably. Down the hall and into Dad's room we had all marched, singing Christmas carols and bearing eggnog. Dad, however, was not conscious enough to know what was happening and we couldn't figure out how to backpedal from our agenda of forced joviality. The whole family felt worse for having tried to do the impossible. For sure, we didn't want to repeat this experience with Mother. Still, Bubba and I agreed that moving the party to her room was the best compromise. One of his daughters and her family would also join us, so altogether there would be eight of us.

Bubba bought a card for Mother to give me, and he called to tell me that she was able to sign it the next day, but barely. Her alertness and spontaneity had vanished and she was exhausted and sleepy again. He had also gotten cards for her to sign for Peggy, and for her younger brother Bill, whose birthday was close. He told me later that he gave her mine last. She had been so groggy signing the others, her handwriting was almost illegible. He waited until she could focus a little better to get her to sign my card. He guessed that this would be the last thing she would write, and he was right.

As it turned out, that weekend Mom got a fresh surge of energy. Friday we met in her room a little before seven o'clock. Alleluia! Mom was not only awake, but enthusiastic and alive in a way I hadn't seen since Christmas. It was wonderful, the best birthday present I could have asked for, to have her *back* again! Her eyes were alight and she was completely alert and responsive to the festive mood.

Kay brought ice cream, a birthday cake for me, and a birthday pie for Peggy. After Peggy and I opened presents and cards, Kay began to serve the refreshments. Mom had not wanted to eat for months, so I had prepared myself not to be disappointed when she excused herself politely. Instead, she asked for cake, pie, *and* ice cream! She was in bed, but in an almost upright position, and she joined in the conversations and laughter. We talked about Peggy's new job, about how hot last summer had been, about Alyssa's day school experiences— none of it very important—and the normalcy of it was wonderful. No new bad news to assimilate. No suppressed grief. No forced joviality to fall flat.

I was not sure how much of her improvement was sheer willpower. Had she had a talk with herself and told herself that she would simply *not* spoil this occasion? That would have been like her. She had told me once of her determination not to let her own grief at her mother's death interfere with Bubba's planned fifth birthday party a day or two after Nana's funeral. My father had suggested they cancel the party, but she had adamantly refused, saying that Bubba would be too disappointed. One just did not let others down on their birthday.

When everyone left an hour or so later, she was very tired and wanted to settle in for the night immediately, but traces of the vitality remained. I gave her a kiss and said to her what I had said since I was a little girl—*Goodnight, I'll see you in the morning.*

❧

Today when I walked into your room
You looked up and smiled at me,
And your eyes sparkled!

Something I'd given up—thought was gone forever—
I get back, if only for a few moments.
I grin back at you. How can I not?!

That old connection—brown eyes to brown eyes—
With the answering sparkle inside:
I love you and I know you love me too!

❧

The next morning when I went over, Mother was still asleep. Dot told me she had fed her a bowl of oatmeal for breakfast, but that Mom went right back to sleep afterwards. I had brought in some papers to grade, so I settled in beside her bed to catch up on grading while still keeping an eye on her. She slept all morning.

When her lunch tray came, I woke her up to see if she was hungry. No, she definitely was not. She said something about making herself eat, even if it didn't taste good.

"Mom," I said, "you don't have to eat this if you don't want it."

"Dot wants me to eat."

"Yeah, that's her job, to try to keep your strength up. But you don't have to eat anything you don't want. Really."

"Oh, well, what is it?"

This was one of those occasions when I could not tell her. Some kind of meat, I thought, but hell if I knew what kind. Some jello. Did she want that?

"No! Too sweet!"

"Potatoes?"

She let me feed her a few bites of potatoes and she drank some milk. I ate the roll that came with her tray and drank her iced tea.

She slept for most of the afternoon.

Around four or five o'clock, another of Mom's granddaughters and her husband walked in, having driven up from Austin. More family arrived and soon the room was full again, as it had been the night before. It seemed we were having another party! Mom's energy increased with the number of family members who dropped in. After awhile she asked that her bed be adjusted so she was sitting upright again; then she smiled and said, "If you all are going to talk in my room, you have to talk loudly enough for me to hear you!" We were delighted to honor her request. If anything, she had more energy now than the night before.

They brought in her supper tray, and Mom glanced at it in disgust.

"Do you want supper?" Kay asked her.

"Not this!"

"What would you like then?"

Mom wasn't sure. I tried to think of things she used to like and suggested pizza to Kay, who relayed the suggestion to Mom. Yes! Pizza would be good for a change! So Bubba and Kay went to find some pizza, the rest of us stayed and talked, and when the pizza arrived, Mom ate a slice or two with obvious enjoyment.

I don't think any of us were naïve enough by this time to think that Mother's improvement was anything other than temporary. Still, we would take what we could get and be thankful for the unexpected blessing of her presence.

I went home on Sunday feeling good about the weekend, and hoping, of course, that this respite could continue for awhile. My only regret about the weekend was that I could not hug her. Leaning over someone in bed for an embrace is inadequate at best. I felt a longing that was to increase over the next weeks to hold her more fully, to put my arms around her for mutual comfort. It didn't occur to me until too late that the only way to achieve that was to have lain down beside her. By the time I thought to do it, she was in too much discomfort to tolerate that kind of contact.

On Tuesday, Bubba's phone message said that Mom's energy was completely spent, that she was again dehydrated, and that she was refusing an IV. He said he had told her that it was her right to refuse it, but that she would probably die in a few days since she wasn't drinking but a few sips of water a day. She said she understood and did not change her mind.

I got to Dallas about five o'clock that next Friday afternoon. Mom was lying flat in the bed, dozing. After a bit, she woke up and saw me, managed a smile, and we exchanged a couple of sentences. I fed her the part of her supper that she wanted, and she went back to dozing. From time to time I would look up from the book I was reading and find her eyes partially open, just looking at my face. It was hard to know what to do. Did she want to talk but lacked the energy? I reached over and rubbed her arm through her satin pajama top. After awhile the aides came in and rolled her over onto her left side.

I wanted to be able to talk with her about her decision to refuse IV's and I was determined to do it without crying. I got up, walked around the floor for a bit, talked with Dot, and got a drink of water. Fortified, I came back in her room. Mom looked up and I thought, *Do it now. She needs to know it's okay with you.* Her left hand was outstretched. I moved the chair up closer and took her hand in both of mine, and looked directly into her eyes. I managed to get through the first two words before I was in tears.

"Mom, it's okay if you don't want to do the IV's. Really, it's okay. We'll miss you a whole lot, but we'll be okay." (Too many okays, I thought to myself, but it didn't seem to matter. She knew what I was trying to say.)

She looked at me sadly and said, "I just . . . can't . . . anymore."

I didn't need her to tell me what it was she couldn't do. She meant everything. She couldn't keep trying to resist the current pulling her downstream. She couldn't keep on struggling. She had used up all of her resources and there was nothing left to draw on.

"I know, Mom. You're so tired. We understand."

I could not let her down by protesting her decision, maybe any more than she could have let me down on my birthday. I did not really want to protest, but my sadness was too deep to cover very effectively.

I swallowed my tears; she was watching me for some kind of cue. What did she need?

What we both needed, I thought, was to lighten the mood before I convinced her I *wasn't* okay.

"Peggy and I were talking about who you want to see first when you get to heaven." Will this work? I smile at her, hoping she can follow me into a lighter mood.

"She bet you would want to see Uncle Ed first, but I said, 'No, first she has to greet Jesus. Gotta do that first. Then her parents, then Uncle Ed and Daddy.'"

Mom smiled a little and closed her eyes. I kept holding her hand and in about five minutes she drifted off to sleep.

The next day she was conscious, but didn't have much to say. She ate very little. Dot managed to talk her into eating some oatmeal for breakfast, but other than that, she took only a few bites. I would ask her from time to time if she was thirsty, and about half the time she said yes. She would want no more than two swallows of water; I think she took it more to please me than because she wanted it. Most of the afternoon she dozed and I read or graded papers. When supper came, she wanted a couple of bites and another sip of water.

I could have stayed longer, there was nothing pressing I needed to do at the cottage, but I didn't feel like my presence helped her much and I was needing time to decompress by myself. Just as I was leaving, I noticed that she was shaking.

"Mom, are you all right? What's wrong?"

No answer.

"Are you hurting, Mom?"

Nothing. Her teeth were chattering.

"What's wrong? Are you cold?"

"Cold! Freezing to death!" She could barely get the words out.

I cover her with another blanket. I look in the hall for the cart that usually holds extra bed linen, but it isn't there. I return to her room and pile on a coat and two robes. By now her body is shaking violently and her skin is white. My agitation spikes and I go to find the charge nurse. Nowhere. She's vanished. Look for an aide, and finally find one tending another resident.

"Do you all have a way to warm up blankets?"

Uncomprehending look.

"I'm sorry to interrupt, but I need to know right now! Do you all have a way to warm blankets, like they do in hospitals?"

"I don't know what you mean. I guess not."

"Do you know where Dot is?"

"Nope."

I go back to Mom's room. Her eyes are closed and her body is now trembling so hard the whole bed shakes. I am amazed she has the strength to tremble like this. This can't be good for her.

She opens her eyes and looks at me. "*Cold.*"

By now I am desperate. I decide to find a nurse on another floor and am heading up the stairs when I see Dot. It's now been ten or fifteen minutes since the shaking began. I convince Dot to check Mom immediately; she is concerned, but doesn't know what else to do.

"How about something hot to drink? Can you all make hot chocolate or hot soup?"

No, they can't. They do have tea bags, and I say I'll take that.

I go back to check on Mom, cover her with two more afghans I find in the closet. Finally Dot comes in with the hot tea, and we try to get Mother to drink some. She takes a couple of swallows, makes a face, and manages to get out, "Terrible soup! Needs some salt!"

I taste it. For tea, it's not bad, but as soup goes, she's right, it is terrible. I get a few more swallows down her and her body slowly begins to relax. Color returns to her face; in about ten more minutes, she has quit shaking and is able to drift off to sleep. I am exhausted. These chills aren't too good for me either.

I had trouble sleeping that night. What if I hadn't been there? Mother was no longer capable of remembering to push the call button even when she was alert; in situations like this, there wasn't a chance that she could have summoned someone. Even if she had, there was no buzzer that rang at the nurses' station, only a light that came on outside her door. It might have taken fifteen minutes or more for the one available aide to see the light on. I wondered if we should get someone to be with her around the clock. I hated leaving her alone, not knowing if she was okay or if someone would notice if she wasn't.

Mom slept most of Sunday. I woke her up at noon to see if she wanted any lunch, and she took a few bites.

She stayed propped up a little in bed for another hour, sometimes awake, sometimes dozing. Several times I looked up from the book I was reading to see her sleepily gazing at my face. I asked if she was okay, and she nodded.

About one o'clock, I showed her a catalog I'd brought. It was a sale catalog put out by one of our favorite manufacturers of women's clothes.

"Want to help me make a decision, Mom? I'm trying to decide how to spend the birthday money you gave me, and I've gotten it down to two dresses. What do you think?"

I stood beside the bed, held the catalog, and showed her the two dresses. She nodded sleepily at both of them. "They're nice."

"Maybe I'll get both!"

She seemed to doze off for a few seconds, but then opened her eyes again.

"Did I give you enough money for both of them?"

"Almost. I'll add a little of my own."

Her eyes closed again and I sat down to continue reading my book. After about ten minutes, Mother stirred in bed and tried to shift her position. I adjusted her pillow for her.

"Let's see that catalog again," she said. She looked through it for a few minutes before putting it down. I think she showed me a dress she liked. I couldn't tell if I had struck a little spark of interest, or if she was trying to make herself pretend interest because she wanted me to feel she still cared about the clothes I chose.

It was hard to know who was trying to please whom, who was doing the giving and who was doing the receiving. I didn't really need help choosing clothes; I took the catalog because I thought it might give her pleasure to repeat this ritual of shopping together we'd done since I was in High School. Whether she did it for me or for herself, she did join in the ritual as much as she could. It didn't matter to either of us, I'm pretty sure, if one or both of us did it primarily to please the other. What mattered was our desire to use this small mutual act to affirm the history of our connection.

On August 9 Mother was diagnosed with another infection. At this point it was called "cellulitis," although later the terms "boil," and "abscess" were also used. This switching of terms was very irritating to me. Did these folks not know what they were doing? According to the medical text I'd gotten, cellulitis was a skin infection almost always caused by either a strep or a staph infection. Antibiotics were the treatment of choice. Boils and abscesses were different altogether. It didn't matter in the long run, however, because on that day Mother made the decision to refuse all medications. Refusing IV's did not seem to be hastening her death, so she took the next logical step. She said she wanted this over, that she was ready to go home.

Dixie Lee and Bubba and I discussed it and agreed that we would of course continue to support her decisions. She was ready to die, and she was making the choices she knew to make that would help her reach that goal. I think that, of the three of us, it may have been easiest for me to automatically support her choice. I had never thought I could or should keep her from dying; I'd defined my role as helping her do what she needed to do. It was much harder for Bubba, who, though his head told him differently, felt that each time he helped her in this way he was killing her.

Dot wanted Bubba's okay to give Mother an antibiotic injection the doctor had ordered for the cellulitis. Caught in the middle of his ambivalence, Bubba agreed to one injection, no more.

Two days later, Dot mentioned casually to me that Mom had had three injections. I asked Bubba about this on his Friday lunch visit. He left the room, and wearing his attorney I-mean-business expression, went immediately to find Dot to get an explanation. Dot was apologetic and promised not to medicate Mom again except for pain-killers.

Friday night I stayed in the room when they got her ready for bed to see what her "cellulitis" looked like. It was an angry reddish/purple swollen area about the size of my palm on the inside of her right hip. It was tender, but the pain was controlled by the Tylenol and Vicadin she had agreed to take. The staff had no idea how Mother had gotten the infection. Transferred from another patient by an aide who didn't use gloves? The result of not cleaning Mother properly? One more unknown, maddening to think about, and so dismissed from our minds as much as possible. There was nothing we could do about it.

In spite of the infection, Mom was in pretty good shape most of that second weekend in August. She was able to carry on a short conversation with me on Friday evening and then again on Saturday afternoon. We talked about a variety of things, none important except for the spontaneous interaction that they signaled.

By the time I got to her room about nine o'clock Sunday morning, however, she was in so much pain from the infection that she was near hysteria. I was unable to get a clear answer from the staff regarding the time she had received her last dose of pain medication—it had been at least twelve hours—but Dot did tell me that the new doctor's orders were that it be given only as requested. No one had told my mother this, and by now she was usually not alert enough to know to ask for more medicine anyway; she just knew that she hurt. I was furious.

I bullied Dot into giving twice the amount of Vicadin ordered, and emphasized that pain needed to be treated in a preventative fashion so that it was not out of control before someone thought to provide the narcotic. I didn't think this should be a new concept to the nursing home staff, but apparently it was. I asked Dot to call the doctor for permission to change the order to around the clock.

Thirty minutes later, Mother was still in extreme pain. Her life-long stoicism in the face of pain had collapsed, and now she was reduced to crying and speaking in monosyllables: *"Hurts! Hurts! Please!"*

I asked her if she thought heat would help but she couldn't concentrate on the question enough to answer. Seeing my mother like this and being unable to help sent my own stress level off the chart. *Do **something**!*

I asked Dot if Mom could use a heating pad. No, that was against policy. How about a hot water bottle? Why, yes! Did they have one? No. Very briefly my memory flashed to the scene in *Terms of Endearment* when Shirley MacLaine, playing the mother of a cancer patient, throws a tantrum at the nurses' station. That would be very, very gratifying, I thought, but managed to restrain myself. Instead, I hurried over to the cottage to get a rubber hot water bottle that I thought I remembered seeing someplace. I found it without too much ado and returned, also taking her heating pad back in case the hot water bottle didn't work. To hell with their policy.

It was easy to get the bottle filled, not so simple to find an aide free who could help me turn Mom to get it positioned right. Eventually, however, we did get it in place and it relieved the pain enough for Mom to calm down and fall asleep within a few minutes. Both of us were exhausted by this time, she from battling the pain, I from the stress of not knowing how to help.

Driving home, I asked myself how I really felt about her dying. Was more under the surface than I was wanting to admit? The answer came, as it sometimes does for me, through a song. A tune I couldn't quite place kept running through my head. What was it? Eventually, I remembered the chorus:

Don't it make you wanna go home, now,
Don't it make you wanna go home?
All God's children get weary when they roam,
Don't it make you wanna go home?

I took that as a tentative answer that I really did understand what she needed to do and could be supportive of her decision.

❧

Until this summer, Mom's stoicism had been as much a part of her personality as her warmth. She was not a complainer.

She once told me a story of an interchange she had with Dad's mother, who had come to visit Mom and Dad a few months after they married. Grandmother's response to pain was the opposite of my mother's: She *never* suffered in silence. Tiny and frail, she had been sickly and pampered all her life, and she expected prompt sympathy as her due. Further, she felt that she should provide an ongoing moment-to-moment account of how and where her pain had increased. Mother put up with Grandmother's perpetual complaints during the week without saying anything, but by Saturday, her patience was wearing thin.

Sunday, Mom woke up with a bad sinus headache, a headache which increased as the day went on. Midafternoon, she was sitting on the side of the bathtub, with a hot wash cloth on the back of her neck and one pressed to her forehead. Walking down the hall, Grandmother looked in the bathroom, saw my mother, and asked, "What's wrong? Do you have a headache?"

"Yes," Mom answered.

"Well, why didn't you say something?"

"Oh," my mom responded, in what may have been the only sarcastic sentence she ever uttered, "I didn't know that would help."

❦

Bubba called Mom's brother Bill and suggested that he come up as soon as possible if he wanted to see Mom again. Bill and his wife Gussie had had their own health problems to deal with, but they were now feeling well enough to make another trip to Dallas. Mother was glad they were coming; she wanted to tell Bill a couple of stories about his childhood that she wasn't sure he knew.

The day they visited was the last "good" day Mom had. She was very sick, very weak, but she was herself again for a couple of hours. Dixie Lee was in Dallas at the time, and told me how the visit went.

While my sister showed Gussie some military records of Edward M., Mom and Bill talked. She told him the stories she'd wanted to relate, and they had time to reminisce a bit. Lunch came, and Dixie Lee helped Mother eat a little. Then she left, leaving Bill sitting beside Mom's bed with Gussie perched on his lap, and the three of them talked about thirty more minutes. Mother told my sister later how good it was to see them.

She had told me the stories about Bill the previous Spring:

One took place right before Christmas when Bill was about three or four. He had diphtheria and was so sick they thought he might die within a day or two. Nana was by his bed, trying to keep him comfortable, when he looked up at her and said, "Nana, if I die, will you hang up my stocking for Santa Claus anyway?" Nana started to cry and said, "Why, baby, *why*?" "So Ed and Dixie can play with my toys," Bill responded, causing his tender-hearted mother to cry harder.

The other story had a somewhat similar tone. Bill was still a small child when he was bitten by a stray dog. He knew that sick dogs were usually shot at the time, out of the fear that they might be rabid. As Nana was dressing the wound, he again brought her to tears by saying, "Nana, if I get rabies, will Daddy shoot me or will the sheriff?"

❦

August 13 was Mother's birthday. She told Bubba not to get her anything. Bubba and Dixie Lee and I talked about it; we all felt bad about ignoring the day, but there was absolutely nothing we could get that seemed appropriate. I had looked for some more brushed-back satin pajamas of the kind she liked, but none was available in August. We all got her cards and I sent some flowers. A mixed bouquet, with plenty of red in it. All of us were in Dallas to celebrate her eighty-ninth birthday.

Mother had by now been put on a mild tranquilizer to ease her agitation, and that, combined with the Vicadin, caused her to sleep through her birthday. We were there, but she did not know it. I tried to show her our cards and the others that had arrived; she was too groggy to focus. On Saturday she woke up once enough to recognize me. I showed her the flowers and held them up to her nose so she could smell them. "Pretty," she said before she fell asleep again.

I left Sunday with no other conversation with her. This process was now hard in two new ways. If she was awake, she was often in significant discomfort that I could not ease, and that was very stressful. If, on the other hand, she slept through my whole visit, I was relieved that she was not in pain but it made me question what purpose my going fulfilled.

My life was again like walking underwater: unable to hurry, unable to hear much, just making one foot follow the other. I was drained, more emotionally than physically. Friday mornings were increasingly difficult, and it was harder to get started on my trip to Dallas. Then I felt guilty for procrastinating. Part of me just didn't want to go back into a situation which I knew could only provide more despair and frustration.

Today I let myself think:
I am so tired—
Layers of fatigue I cannot sleep away,
Feelings of anger and worry and hopelessness I cannot shake.
Why, after all, am I still doing this?

A long, long pause as I wait for my answer:
I guess this must be commitment. I go,
Not because she can give anything back, and
Surely not out of duty, and
Not even because I can make much difference.
I go because I belong there.

Similarly:
I guess this is love.
Some bond so deep, so natural an element,
I cannot negotiate it.
We are connected, she and I,
Past all reason, past fatigue, past priorities.

Ultimately:
I go because I cannot stay away and still be me.

Someone in the family suggested to me in August that perhaps the stress was making me a bit irritable, a charge I hotly denied. I was not aware of irritability and it annoyed me that someone would dream that up. What I was aware of was that:

- red lights were taking twice as long to change.
- other drivers were suddenly more inconsiderate. What were they doing on the road anyway?
- the lines in the grocery store were longer and the checkers were much slower than they had been just a month before.
- someone must have given my phone number to a national network of telephone solicitors.

It was hard enough to have to contend with the universe inexplicably turning against me without also having to defend myself against unfair accusations of irritability!

By August, Bubba had sketched out an obituary. I had made a couple of suggestions and that task was taken care of. I thought about what I would wear to the funeral. All white, maybe, with red accessories?

Mother had said she wanted "Swing Low, Sweet Chariot" sung at the service. In addition to finding the song comforting, I knew that she was remembering that it had been sung at her father's cemetery service. As a community leader in the early 1900s, he had fought hard to make sure that the African-American children had a brick school. He had exposed secret KKK political contributions. He had given Blacks as well as Whites credit at his meat market during the Depression until he finally ran out of money himself and had to close down the market. Professor Greer, the superintendent of the Black schools in El Campo and the church choir director, had approached my Uncle Ed after my grandfather's death to ask if his choir could show their respect for him by singing at the cemetery. They did "Going Home" by Dvorak, and "Swing Low."

I knew Mother would prefer not to have a White singer doing that song. I decided not to worry about possible racism and just do what she wanted. While I pondered off and on about whom to ask, the words ran through my head and provided comfort:

Swing low, sweet chariot
Comin' for to carry me home
Swing low, sweet chariot
Comin' for to carry me home

I looked over Jordan and what did I see
Comin' for to carry me home
A band of angels comin' after me
Comin' for to carry me home

One of the other things I did in August was to find a printing company in Bryan that could print the kind of card I had in mind for notifying Mom's friends and relatives of her death. I'd decided to put a picture of her taken when she was ten on the front; inside, I wanted to excerpt an autobiographical piece she'd written in 1998 for a Creative Writing class she was taking.

❦

Who Is Dixie?

Was she the sun-bronzed child with dark hair flying who "skinned the cat" on the trapeze bar or played in the rain and squished mud between her toes? Or was she the teenager who clattered down the winding stairs to elude the clutches of an older brother? Could she have been the young woman for whom Christmas was so meaningful that she chose it for her wedding day? Or was she, perhaps, the young mother who sang as she waltzed her babies about the room? Was she the High School math teacher who, without interrupting her explanation, caught the eye of a recalcitrant student and gave a slight shake of her head? Or was Dixie the elderly woman who stood at the open casket of her husband, took a deep breath, blinked away her tears and turned to greet a guest with a smile?

❦

We continued to be concerned that Mom's pain and agitation were not being controlled by the medication ordered by the nursing home physician. We knew that hospice was committed to a more aggressive treatment of pain, and we decided that we would try again to get them involved with Mother's case.

This attempt worked no better than the one in the Spring. My brother was there when the hospice representative visited Mom, and he told me later what transpired. The representative told my mother that hospice would be available to help with the weeks or months she had left. Upon hearing that, Mom fell apart. She was counting on hours or days, not weeks or months. Bubba said she turned away, trying to keep him from seeing her cry, but could not calm herself. Upset that she was so upset, Bubba turned to the hospice worker and said, "I don't know what to do. . ."

Trying to help, she touched Mother's arm and said, "You're frustrated." That was a vast understatement, and seemed only to increase Mom's agitation.

Eventually the representative left. Unable to get Mom calm, my brother asked Dot to give her a sedative and then he called Mom's minister, Sandy. He was told that Sandy was in a meeting and he responded by asking the receptionist to interrupt him, that this was an emergency. Sandy left his meeting and came right out.

He was exactly the right person for my brother to call. Mother had always been close to her ministers, and she was especially fond of Sandy. She liked him, she liked his Scottish brogue, and she felt understood by him. Further, I've realized in retrospect, this must have been a spiritual crisis for her: feeling abandoned by God for the first time in her life. Why wasn't God letting her die? Her minister was the one who could help.

At her funeral, Sandy referred back to this visit. He told us that Mom had told him how much she needed to die and had asked why it was taking so long. His response was perfect: "Dixie, folks like you know *where* they are going, they just don't know *when*." I don't know what else he said. Did he talk about Jesus also feeling abandoned by God as he was dying? I'm sure Sandy prayed with her and that that helped her. By the time he left, she was relatively composed, and did not again feel this agonizing level of agitation. She had been reminded that she was, after all, going home.

Mom's desperation to go home had to become something I supported. How could I support her and not what she most desired? While my own beliefs were less specific and certain than hers, I hoped *for her* that she was right, that before long she would soon be with loved ones who could comfort her and take her home.

At about this time I found in the cottage another packet of letters that Mom had saved through the years. The more recent things were on the top, so as I read them I traveled backward in time. There were letters and cards from the three of us children, a hand-drawn Mother's Day card I had given her when I was in the third grade, and letters to her from my father when they were courting.

I found two short letters to her written by her father when she was a child visiting her grandparents. And then I found one more from her dad, mailed to her address at the University of Texas. in 1929. It was a response to a letter that she had written him on his sixty-eighth birthday. He wrote that getting older did not bother him; he felt "no terror at being alone as the eastern horizon recedes." The next line was the one that made me stop, reread it, and put the letter on top of the stack so I would know where to find it later.

Still on the theme of dying, my grandfather had written to his eighteen-year old daughter: "As for that great adventure beyond, that only means that me and the angels will be a little lonesome until my own folks are gathered home."

I knew that Mom had trusted her father implicitly; if he said something, she could count on it. From my own perspective of one generation and seventy years later, I was unsure how much of his deepest beliefs this rather poetic phrasing captured. Some, but not all, of his thinking, I suspected. But without a doubt this was the part he wanted to pass on to his daughter, his Gal-baby, his Dixie-girl. He was, after all, nearly seventy and might die relatively soon.

It was a lovely thought: that not just he, but the angels too, would be lonely until she was "gathered home." There was something about that verb that touched me. It implied more than *coming* home. *Gathered* sounded warmer, cozier: Someone would be reaching out to gently bring her safely home. She would not have to do it alone. Like a lighthouse, I thought, steadily shining its beam, night after night, so that lost ships could make it back home.

I imagined her father sitting at their diningroom table in El Campo all those years ago, wondering what to say to give his daughter something to hold onto for comfort when he died. Something that would not alarm her when she read it, but that she could keep for later. She had kept it for seventy years.

❦

I went back to Dallas the next Friday, August 20 The infection had subsided a bit, and Mom was on less painkiller and so easier to wake up. She had had nothing at all to eat since August 14 and only a few sips of water a day. How could she still be alive? All of her muscles were atrophying. She could still move her hands up to her face and she could sometimes open her eyes partway. She had difficulty swallowing even small amounts of liquid and usually coughed and choked. I didn't know people could be so weak and still live.

Her voice, when she did try to speak, was very soft. Hardly able to smile anymore, she raised her eyebrows to show recognition and affirmation. With her eyes closed, she was unable to lip read, so she missed much of what was said to her.

When I got there, I kissed her as usual on the forehead and said,

"Hi, Mom, it's Donna. I love you." She opened her eyes a little and said, "I love you" back to me. I asked if she was okay and she gave a tiny nod and raised her eyebrows. I sat beside her and held her hand as waves of sadness rolled through me. It was so *hard* to see her like this and be unable to help at all. After she fell back asleep, I looked through cards she had received.

About twenty minutes later, she opened her eyes and spoke again. She had rehearsed what she wanted to say: "Do you suppose they would let me wear a diaper tonight instead of just wetting the bed?" This was the longest sentence she had said in weeks. She phrased requests with this kind of nonchalance only when she wanted something so badly that she was afraid that I would feel terrible if I couldn't make it happen. It was her way of protecting both of us, of showing me that she could handle a "no" and that I shouldn't feel responsible.

Since her infection began, they had refused to let her wear diapers in order that "more air could get to the infection." It was another policy decision which made no sense to me and which made life harder for my mother. Lying on her back, as she did all the time now, no air could get to the infection anyway. Beside, she was dying. Who cared if they could clear up the infection, as long as they controlled her pain? I hated that she should have to worry about this on top of everything else that was happening to her.

I told Mother I would ask. I walked to the nurses' station about fifty feet away to talk to the nurse on duty. By the time I got there, I had decided that shameless manipulation was the only path to take.

"Excuse me," I said, "Mother wants me to ask you if she can't please wear a diaper tonight. She said you'd understand."

The nurse looked torn. "It's against doctor's orders."

"I know, but Mom said you could understand how important it was to her even though the doctor couldn't."

She closed her eyes, took a deep breath, and turned to unlock the door where the diapers were kept.

I went back to Mom's room and told her that an aide would be in right away, that the nurse had agreed to the diaper. She answered with a small smile and a soft, "Oh, I'm so glad."

I admit to some guilt at violating policy. The nurse would be held responsible if the doctor found out, and doctors do not like nurses' violating their orders. I liked her a lot and hated that I might get her into trouble, but my first priority was always my mother.

Mom slept fairly well that night. Most of Saturday she dozed. I sat close to her bed and watched her and occasionally read a little. Several times she had a startle response: her hands would suddenly reach out and her face would contort as she made a low cry. It looked like nightmares to me; I would stand up, tell her she was okay, and take her hands or stroke her hair until she seemed peaceful again. When she was awake, I offered her a sip of water, on which she often choked. I stayed beside her and watched her sleep and hoped with her that this would be over soon.

About nine P.M., I collected Mom's laundry to take back to the cottage to wash, and leaned over to say goodbye just as Dot walked in the room.

"Goodnight, Mom. I'm going over to the cottage now. I'll see you in the morning."

Mother opened her eyes and looked at me with more wistful-ness than I had ever seen in her face. "Oh, honey," she said softly, "I *wish* I could go with you." Her eyes filled with tears, and mine did too in instant resonance. "There are still so many things I want to do. . ."

It was hard to get the words out. "I know, Mom, I know." I kissed her and went into the hall, Dot behind me. She walked me to the outside door and held me while I cried. It was the feeling I'd had about Mom's missing the birthday party. It was hard to be with her when she wasn't *there*, but it was heartbreaking to be with her when she wanted something she knew she couldn't have.

Sunday morning she slept, but it was a troubled sleep. I was not sure if she was uncomfortable physically or if she was dreaming. Were these dreams? Was this delirium? Hallucinations? Since she couldn't answer questions, I had no way to find out. Whatever they were, they didn't help. I asked for the doctor to be called to authorize an increase in Ativan, the tranquilizer she was taking.

By Sunday afternoon, her distress had increased. Her face often crumpled like a child's about to sob, and she cried out incoherently. I was unable to understand much of what she said, but I tried to comfort her by stroking her forehead and hair, and reassuring her that we would take care of anything that was wrong. I think she heard me, but I was not much help to her.

She became more upset, calling out more loudly. Something about a baby was upsetting her.

"The baby, the baby!" she cried out in great agitation.

"Mom, are you worried about your baby?"

Her faced relaxed and she nodded. *Finally* somebody understood her! Soon, however, she was upset again; being understood was not enough.

"Mom, *I* have the baby. It's okay, I'll take care of the baby. Nothing can happen to her." (*Is the baby female?*). "She's safe now, she's okay. I'm taking the baby home with me."

Mom heard me and grew calm again.

I stood by her bed and smoothed her hair until I had to start my drive back to Bryan. I hated leaving her like this. Most of the time no one was in her room to hear her; she might be feeling this desperate for an hour before anyone knew.

Before I left, I said to her, "Bye, Mom. I love you. I'll see you next weekend." She was alert enough to nod a little, but looked at me dubiously; she was not sure she would be there next weekend.

I talked to Dot about her medication. Clearly, whatever she was taking was not holding the agitation. Maybe Ativan was not the tranquilizer for her?

❦

The drive back to Bryan took the usual two hours and forty-five minutes. I needed to get back to my own home, my own routine, but I felt terrible about leaving Mom so easily upset. She had had no food in over a week, and only a few swallows of water a day, and she'd been dehydrated for weeks before. How much longer could this go on?

I thought back to the baby interaction. She had felt so desperate until I'd said that I had the baby and would take care of her. My mind kept circling the interaction; there was something about it I needed to understand.

Oh, Lord, I get it.

From out of nowhere, I remembered the age regression I had done with Earl in the hypnotherapy workshop several years before. I had been the baby whom Mother carried around all day until I was comforted. In a very real way, Mom was telling me now that she couldn't take care of the baby anymore, and she couldn't rest until I'd said I would bring her home and take care of her myself.

I let that idea settle for awhile—this was important, I didn't want it to slip away—and then I thought about it more objectively. What Mother and I had enacted was, in fact, a developmental process considered by many psychologists as crucial for healthy autonomy. A child is comforted and soothed by a caregiver and eventually internalizes the nurturing ability enough to learn to comfort herself or himself. We can let our mothers go, give up our clinging, when we have learned that they are not the only source of comfort. We are not left alone, we have someone inside to comfort us. This leaves us freer to be adventurous and more self-confident in relationships and work; if things don't work out, we can turn to ourselves for healing.

My mind flashed back to something someone had said at a therapy workshop I'd attended the previous Fall when I was on Sabbatical. We had been talking about the mother/daughter bond, and how important that was to most women. During a break, I heard someone say, "Daughters of good mothers are never alone."

Daughters of good mothers are never alone.

I had told Mother I would take care of the baby, and I had never broken a promise to her. In my mind's eye I had an image of my mother—younger than now, and healthy—holding a baby that she loved, and then carefully handing her over to me. *Okay, Mom. Okay, I'll take care of the baby.*

❦

On August 24, Mom came back for awhile. As my brother related the story, Dot and the nursing home doctor were in her room that afternoon, discussing her case. Mom looked at Dot and said, "I want to get up."

Dot turned to the doctor for confirmation that Mother was too weak to be sitting up. Mother used her authoritative tone of voice: "In *that* chair, Dot. *Now.*"

So they moved her to the recliner, tilted her so she was almost horizontal, and tucked her in. Mother said, "Now I want a big glass of very cold water."

Completely caught off guard, Dot protested, "But, Dixie, you haven't wanted cold water since you got here!"

"I want it now. With ice."

Dot blinked and then turned to get the water, and Mom called, "Also ice cream. Make it vanilla!"

Bubba and I knew that this return of Mom's self was only temporary. But it was so wonderful to have her back for a few minutes!

❦

The last weekend in August my cousin Edward flew down from Virginia to see Mom. He was flying into the Dallas airport and I was supposed to meet his plane. I stopped by the nursing home on my way into town and found Mother much weaker than she had been when I'd seen her the previous weekend. It had now been two weeks since she had taken any food, and she was taking no more than an ounce of water a day. Her mind seemed cloudy, although it was hard to tell how cloudy because she talked so little. I bent over, kissed her, and told her I would be picking up Edward and bringing him to her room. I was not sure she heard me, or if she did, if she could track what I was saying. There was only the shadow of her presence that weekend, no more.

I picked up Edward and we went back to Mom's room for him to visit with her. I had warned him how very ill she was, but it was hard to convey her lack of focus. When we got there, he said to her, "Hi, Aunt Dixie!" She either didn't hear him or didn't have the energy to open her eyes. "Mom," I said more loudly to her, "Edward's here." She opened her eyes very slightly. I scooted down so I was in her line of vision. "Mom, it's Edward." He took my place so she could see his face. She gave him a long, bleary look. "Well," she finally said, "I'll . . . be . . . darned." This was not the most enthusiastic greeting he'd ever received, but I guess it beat his mom's on that Easter, years before.

She said very little else that was coherent that weekend. She was in a different state now, or perhaps on the edge of a different state that would intensify in the following week. She was not exactly asleep; it was more as if she were in a drug-induced fog. I stayed by her bed most of time while Edward went back and forth to the cottage. She was agitated, not crying out like she had the previous weekend, but arching her back (was the spinal stenosis causing pain again?), pushing back her covers, frowning and moaning softly. She seemed to be in the same mental state she had been in the Sunday before—dreaming or delirious or whatever it was—but it was harder to calm her down. She had so little attention to give to the outside world that it was hard to break through the fog, even to provide comfort. Sunday morning she seemed more physically uncomfortable. Each time the aides rolled her to her side, either side now, she cried out in pain. Her back seemed to be hurting her but she couldn't get comfortable on her side either.

Sunday afternoon she was trying to communicate something with a great deal of urgency; her words were too garbled for me to understand. She knew that something was wrong physiologically with her speech, and cried out, "I can't talk! I can't talk!" All I could answer was, "It's okay, Mom, I can understand most of what you try to say." Her agitation decreased a bit. Her favorite aide, Gloria, came into the room and she relaxed a bit more. She trusted both Gloria's skill and her caring. As long as Gloria was on duty, she felt safe.

I waited until Mom was coherent again before leaving to drive home. I leaned over as usual and said, "I'm leaving now, Mom. I love you." She could barely open her eyes, but she tried, and then she whispered, "Love you." This time when I left, I did something I had rarely done since I was a little girl: I kissed her on the lips. She was able to make a very tiny pursing response as she tried to kiss me back.

Two days later, Tuesday, August 31, Bubba called to say that Dot thought that Mom would probably die that day. I said I was on my way. I dropped my dog at the vet's, called patients to cancel appointments, and made sure that students showing up for my classes this first week of the Fall semester would be met by someone. I was packed and on the road within an hour. Having rushed to get started, I realized after about twenty-five miles that I was not in that much of a hurry after all to face what Dallas would have to offer this time. I almost stopped at a vegetable stand by the highway, and had to smile at how transparent my ambivalence was. I wanted very much to be with Mother, and I also wanted very much not to jump into this last part of the process. I remembered having the same mix of feelings when I was in labor on my way to the hospital. There was an acute sense in both situations of knowing that my life would never be the same again, that something irrevocable was about to take place at a pace faster than I was comfortable with.

As I drove through the small towns between Hearne and Waco, the words kept repeating in my head that this would be the last time I would be making this trip to see Mom. The route that I knew so well that I could drive it almost with my eyes closed would no longer be part of my routine life. If I didn't stop now or on the way back to read the historical markers beside the road, I might never read them. My mind felt as if it were in slow motion, recording the details for some future reference. There was the old two-room schoolhouse beside the highway, falling apart. There was the big white mansion on the Marlin bypass. There was the little grocery store where I bought ice cream sandwiches.

Dixie Lee was already in Dallas with Mom, and Bubba had taken off work. The three of us met in Mother's room and then talked with Dot about what signs might signify impending death and what we should expect. Mom was moving a little less than she had two days before, and she now seemed completely unable to respond to the outside world. There was a strange odor about her, probably the result of failing liver. Her eyes never opened and she gave no indication that she knew we were there. I had the sense that she was so immersed in her own internal world that she had no energy at all to pay attention to what was happening on the outside. The three of us stayed by her bed for several hours and saw no change.

In the early evening I told my brother and sister that I wanted to stay with her that night. I did not know if they also did, but if not, I would be glad to stay and call them if there was a change. They had been with her all day and decided to leave then: Bubba to drive to his home in north Dallas, and Dixie Lee to go over to the cottage.

In retrospect, this night was when I really said goodbye. The minutes and hours of my time by her bed that night are very clear to me. After Tuesday night/early Wednesday morning, the days became a blur and only specific incidents now stand out. But that first night is crystalline in my memory.

The lights were turned out in the hall at nine, and since her room door was always propped open, her room darkened substantially. I turned off the hospital light over her bed. Only the lamp Peggy had brought over from the cottage was still on. I had grown up with that lamp in our livingroom, and having it in the room with me that night provided a small amount of familiar coziness. I pulled the recliner up to Mom's bed. It was much more comfortable than the straight chair also in her room, but it was deep enough that it necessitated getting up and standing to reach Mom. To the left of her bed was a bedside table, and in its top drawer were the old portraits and photographs of Mom from infancy through young adulthood. On the wall on her right was the painting she had done of "Home." These details always come back when I think of being with my dying mother, probably because I looked at them in a different way that night.

Mom became restless, as she had been Sunday, but in a more subdued way. Perhaps every fifteen or twenty minutes she roused from a state of apparent ease—peaceful expression, not moving around, not vocalizing—to frowning and moving her hands and trying to shift her position. Sometimes during these more restless spells, she made small sounds. I found that when I stood up and took her hands or touched her face and reassured her during these periods of greater agitation she could settle back down into calmness. I tried once *not* standing up, wanting to see how long it would take before Mom calmed herself; I discovered that it was impossible for me to wait. My instinctive need to stand and help her was in charge that night.

Every time I stroked Mom's brow that night, her eyebrows lifted, as they used to when she smiled. Too weak to smile, she could still indicate a pleasant awareness of what was happening. All night, each time I stroked her face, her eyebrows lifted in acknowledgement. Once I moved my hand down to touch the side of her cheek and chin, and she smiled! It was a very tiny smile, but unmistakable. After that, when I got up to calm her, I repeated the whole gesture. Each time, she raised her eyebrows and smiled very slightly. I wondered whom it reminded her of. Nana? Daddy?

Aides came and went; when they turned Mom to check the infection, she groaned. Clearly, she could still feel pain. Other than those times, however, as the night went on, she quit making any sounds at all.

Sometime around midnight, it became important to me to know if she knew I was the one who was with her. I kissed her forehead and smoothed her hair, and I called, "Mom, it's Donna. It's Donna, Mom. I love you." I had the impression she had to swim back to the surface from the great depth that was now where she lived. Did some part of her awareness remember her calling Aunt Em? "Mom, it's Donna. Can you hear me?"

She gave an almost imperceptible nod. She knew. It was her last gift to me, our last undeniable connection. Tears flooded my eyes from a variety of feelings: gratitude for her responding, a deep aching sense of loss, love, and something else I couldn't name.

Now, months later, it is this small piece of time that I think of when I need to feel the constancy of her love. I was to have a smorgasbord of other feelings that week, from horror to laughter, but it was this last response from Mother to me that touched me most profoundly.

Between one and two o'clock Mom seemed to be sleeping peacefully. I could still feel wisps of her presence, like perfume lingers after a woman walks past. Her colors, having begun fading in January, were now nearly gone. I thought as I sat by her bed watching her of how I had described our relationship once: As if we were colored lights, I explained—she a rich rose, and I a dark aqua—lights that blended into a beautiful shade of purple. While I could blend in wonderful ways with other people, only the mix of Mom and me gave that specific, cherished shade. The color she and I made together was irreproducible, and although I knew there were lots of other lovely blends, I hated to give up ours after having loved it and lived in it for so long.

As Mom rested quietly, I also thought a lot about Gary's dream of his father, in which he was able to see his father across his dad's whole lifetime. Gary did this after a parent's death; I wondered if I could do it before. The foundation was there. I had come to know and appreciate Mom as a young girl and young woman as I went through photographs and portraits, and as I listened to Mom tell stories about those years. My own memories provided the basis for understanding her continued development from age forty through this final year of her life. Could I put it all together and now see her as all of those ages, as real to me when she was ten or thirty as she was now at age eighty-nine?

I opened the drawer of the bedside table and began looking at photographs, connecting with what I understood of Dixie at all these ages. Although they looked very different, the hands that showed in this picture of her taken when she was two were the same hands that rested on the blanket in front of me. The eyes were the same, hadn't even changed much. Her body had gotten old; it seemed to me that her spirit had not. She was still in the midst of evolving when Prednisone short-circuited the process. This paradox of ageless spirit and aging body began to feel more undeniable to me as I looked back and forth from early pictures of her to the Mom in bed.

I remembered a story my Aunt Jimmie told me once about my grandfather. She asked him once what *his* father, Edward M., died of: heart attack, or stroke, or what? She said my grandfather turned on her and said in an offended tone of voice, as if it were an insult to imply that his father might succumb to an ordinary illness, "Why, he didn't die *of* anything! He just wore out!" It felt to me, also, that Mom's body simply wore out; it couldn't keep on going with so many parts functioning poorly. Her spirit was a different matter altogether.

I looked at the clock. It was now two-thirty. I was tired and a little sleepy by this time. My mind kicked the traces of linear thinking, and began to drift, sometimes looking at Mother's painting of her El Campo home, and imagining her running out the front door to school, doing homework at the oak table, falling asleep in her bedroom, talking with a brother on the upstairs sleeping porch. I could see her wonderful smile light up the room whether she was in an El Campo Presbyterian Sunday School, or at a dance in college, or welcoming a child home from school. Memories and images tumbled together. Like a stained glass window, each piece had its separate identity and beauty, but it also contributed to the picture as a whole. All of this, all of Mother, was in the process of undergoing a transformation. I knew what she hoped was on the other side of her dying. What did I hope for on her behalf?

If my wish could make it happen, I answered myself, I would wish for exactly what she did. I wanted her to be able to go home, to be again with people who loved her. I wanted all of the Dixies, across all the years, to feel welcomed, not just the elderly, very sick woman in front of me. I wanted all the life that she had experienced to come together in *one* Dixie, with the whole being more than the sum of the parts. And I wanted her to feel like she was home, a home that included the house where she grew up, but might include much more also. I closed my eyes and imagined this cumulative Dixie set free of her body, able to step outside of time and other worldly constraints. Free to drift and touch people and places from her past that were now somehow alive in whatever dimension her spirit would live. Free also to move with these loved ones into a timeless future.

The yearning underneath my hopes seemed to dim everything else. For this period of time, nothing else mattered, and I channeled all of my energy into hoping, almost as if the hopes themselves could provide a bridge for her into some new plane.

I studied again her painting of her childhood home. I imagined this complete Dixie filled with joy as she rushed in her front door, delighting in all the associations of that home that she had been unable to touch since her parents died and the home burned. This was fantasy, I knew, but I hoped that in some way I could not understand, it might also be her reality. I did not need to know that night, nor have I asked myself since, where exactly Mom was going, if anywhere. I know where I hope she is, and that is enough.

She became restless and as I stood to comfort her again, all the songs about home I had been collecting somewhere in my mind suddenly sprang forth. Standing beside her and smoothing her hair back from her forehead, I sang them all to her: spirituals her father wrote about heaven and the one about the old wooden spout; "Swing Low, Sweet Chariot"; Mary Chapin Carpenter's song with its wonderful lyric that seemed like it was written for tonight, "I'm just resting in the arms of the great wide open/ Gonna pull my soul in/ And I'm almost home." I sang the song Holly Near recorded to let Mom know that I knew she wasn't really going to leave me. The third verse to "Amazing Grace" came out in the second person: "Through many dangers, toils, and snares/ You have already come/ 'Twas grace that brought you safe thus far/ And grace will lead you home." I remembered the haunting arrangement of the gospel hymn "Jesus is Calling" in the opening credits to the movie *Trip to Bountiful* (filmed near El Campo), and I sang that also: "See on the portals he's waiting and watching/ Calling 'Oh, sinner, come home.'" Words to a lullaby for the very young Dixie danced around in my mind and came out in song fragments to a melody I had written years before. I decided that later I would ask my cousin Edward to come up with better music, but for now, this was good enough.

I am not sure that she heard me. I was singing pretty softly, standing there by her bed and smoothing her hair back from her forehead. It was night and all the residents' doors were open; I didn't want to disturb them. Still, she was wearing her hearing aids, and while I was having all of these other grand hopes for her, hoping also that she could hear me that night seemed like a small enough addition. Maybe, the way her father recognized her in the doorway when he was dying, even though he was nearly blind, she could recognize my voice and the songs even though she could barely hear. Somehow, it didn't much matter. I needed to sing to her, whether she could hear or not.

I sang to her most of the night. Once a male aide I had never seen before came in to check on her. He was in tears as he told me how he wished he had sung to his dying father like this; he just hadn't thought to do it at the time. I told him maybe it wasn't too late.

As the sky began to lighten with morning, I kissed Mom and got ready to go to the cottage. I was tired. Something felt completed inside me and also between me and Mother. I needed to get some sleep, and, for the moment, I was all sung out.

❦

Dixie-Girl, a Lullaby
The morning's cool and the breeze is soft
And there's sunshine on your face
You can close your eyes and drift through time
Days touched by love and grace

Remember how you ran so free
Dark hair flying loose
You can fly again—let go and soar—
Touch earth and heaven too

Look who's here to take you home
See the joy you bring
Your father sang goodbye to you
And again he's here to sing

"Come home, my little Dixie-girl
It's time to come on home
Come fly with us as we go on
My little girl, my precious one"

Mom did not die until Sunday night. In those days of extended vigil, there are only a few specifics that stand out in my mind.

Thursday night, I think, I was with Mother again in the early morning hours. Two night aides whom I had never met were on duty and had come in twice to check on Mom. About three o'clock they came in again. I had been singing to Mom, as I did off and on all week whenever I was alone with her, and they waited in the hall until I'd finished a song before asking to check Mom's bedding. I backed out of the way and stood a few feet from the foot of the bed, almost physically holding myself back. I was afraid they would hurt her. She had made no sound since Tuesday night, and I told myself as I backed away that she was probably in some other dimension, beyond pain. When they rolled her to her right side, though, a very deep, long moan came from what seemed like the depths of her being. I had never heard her—or anyone—make that sound, and my tight hold on self-possession crumbled. It sounded to me that she was in terrible pain; I had to fight the desire to keep from interfering with the aides in some forceful way. Tears poured down my face, and I held my fingers over my mouth to keep from sobbing aloud.

The aides were actually quite gentle with her, and were able to change the pad efficiently and with a minimum of jostling her. As they turned to leave, one of them stopped. She came over, put her arms around me and said, "I'm sorry. Let me give you a hug." Hers was such an unexpected reaching out to me that whatever remnant of defenses I still had in place disappeared. I held onto her and cried for awhile before I could get back in control.

A segment of another night, probably Friday, stands out in my mind. Dixie Lee and Bubba and I were all in the room. Mother's breathing was a desperate attempt to get air in her lungs. She was gasping, using her diaphragm to help, I assumed because her chest muscles were by now too atrophied to do the job. About every five minutes, she groaned as she exhaled. My internal alarm messages were desperate: *Help her, help her! Get her some oxygen! Start the IV again! You've got to do **something!***

This was the first time that I could not follow my instinctive need to respond to her body in distress. Before, if she was cold or in pain or agitated, I could try to address the problem. I might fail, but at least I could try. But this time if I followed my desire to help it would surely postpone her death, and she hadn't wanted that. By keeping my hands clasped tightly in my lap and my mind slightly out of focus, I managed to sit quietly. I remember thinking it felt like being in transitional labor: *Don't push, don't push!*, when every possible instinct demanded that response. This was to be the last, and hardest, thing that I had to do: keeping myself from intervening when each moment I waited demanded immediate action. Peggy, drawing on her years of nursing experience in intensive care, had told me that it was hard to kill someone. I was seeing for myself that the body sometimes keeps fighting long past the time it should have stopped if logic had anything to do with it.

We, Mom's children, sat beside her, not talking, watching her body struggle to live. My brother looked up and said sadly, "She never was very good at quitting." Yes, that was it. Consciously she may have wished for death weeks before, but someone had forgotten to notify her unconscious. It was still operating on her "Keep on keeping on" lifelong motto.

In the blur of that week, I also remember Dot, and Gloria, Mom's favorite aide. Dot truly loved Mom. Each time she left the room after doing what she could to help, there were tears in her eyes: Her beloved Dixie was slipping away. Gloria was less emotional, but incredibly respectful of Mother. She always talked to her, just in case Mom could hear, telling her what she was about to do, and then she watched Mom's face for signals of pain. Often she stayed to talk to me for a few minutes, asking some question about what Mom used to be like. One time, upon seeing the pictures of Mom taken when she was young, she called all the floor staff together to show them too. Mother was clearly much more to her than an old woman near death.

Mother died at 6:30 P.M., Sunday, September 5. That morning she had been peaceful, breathing very lightly. We had given up predicting when she would die. I needed to go home to see a couple of patients I was worried about and to make arrangements for someone to cover my next week's classes, so decided to risk an overnight trip to Bryan; I would be back by mid-morning Monday, earlier if necessary. I called my patients to set up the appointments and headed back to Bryan.

My appointments were scheduled for seven and eight that night. At 6:40, I called the nursing home again to see if Mom was still stable. Dot answered the phone. Rather than answering me, she said she would let me talk to Bubba, who was standing there at the nurses' station.

Mom had just died, he said. Dot and Gloria had been with her, and her death was peaceful. The doctor was on her way out. The funeral would not be until Tuesday, so Bubba suggested that I not come back to Dallas until the next morning.

Somehow, and incomprehensibly, it seemed so sudden! The seesaw, which had been balanced so precariously this last week between life and death, had tipped. It was just a small change, but before she had been alive, and now she wasn't. I could not quite wrap my mind around it.

I agreed to come the next day and hung up the phone. What should I do? Could I possibly get through two therapy sessions, having just been told my mother had died? Surely I should cancel them!

After all these years of dreading her death, the moment was here. *What*, I asked myself, *are you feeling?* Nothing that I'd anticipated: nine-tenths calmness, one-tenth unnamed distress. No panic, no anger, no guilt. No tears for now. It was over.

I saw my patients. I was probably a bit distracted, but I hope they got their money's worth.

Monday afternoon, Labor Day, my brother and I went to the church to plan the funeral with Sandy. I knew that Mother had told him what she wanted, and I expected that there would be few details to work out. Unfortunately, this was not a good day for Sandy. He seemed annoyed, perhaps because it was Labor Day and he had counted on a holiday. There was no expression of sympathy, no warmth, just an abrupt let's-get-this-over-with manner. He let me know immediately that Sarah Cramer would not be allowed to play the recessional, regardless of arrangements made months before. It would be an insult to his organist. Further, the service would be out of balance with so many songs, so some needed to be cut or shortened. I had had no preconception that Presbyterian ministers were proprietary about how their funerals were conducted. Low on emotional reserves, I was battling my intense desire to walk out when Bubba stepped in to help. We finally agreed to a service of Sandy's liking.

Tuesday morning I picked up a corsage for Mom: pink, as she'd requested, but with the tiniest sliver of red ribbon. I took it by the funeral home and asked to see her. I had wondered how I would react, what feelings would arise, when I saw her body in the casket. I felt very little. Her body looked fine, much better, in fact, than she had looked in weeks. *She* was not there.

I gave the gentleman assisting me the corsage, and he pinned it on her lapel.

I took another look at her body and remembered something.

"I'm sorry," I said politely, "you're going to have to poof her."

"Excuse me?!" Eyebrows raised to his hairline.

"I'm afraid she's a bit too flat-chested. You'll need to poof her up."

There was a silence as he stared at me in stunned bewilderment. I fixed him with my brightest smile and waited. Finally his face cleared, and he bowed his head in formal deference.

"If you'll excuse me, I believe we can poof your mother."

They did a nice job; I didn't ask how. Mom would have been pleased.

❦

Two of Mother's friends furnished lunch at the cottage for the extended family, and then we got dressed for the service. My nieces persuaded me to wear turquoise instead of the red accessories I had planned on with my white dress.

Mom's funeral was beautiful. The bulletins were exactly as she and I had worked out in June; we sang selected verses of the songs that she had wanted. Sandy came through with a gracious and comforting message, and four of Mother's grandchildren offered brief memories. Best of all was Iva, the friend of a friend I had found to sing "Swing Low, Sweet Chariot." She had a wonderful, rich contralto voice, and she sang the spiritual slowly and with just the right amount of emotion. It was as if Mom was singing through her, reassuring us that she'd made it home.

The service was not doleful, and I think it did succeed in helping my mother leave on the note of triumph she had wanted.

❦

The burial was to be the next morning in Edna, a town about thirty-five miles from El Campo, where my father had grown up and was buried. The fourteen of us family members drove down in several cars. It was quite a way there, and I was glad to have Peggy in the car with me.

As always, conversation between the two of us flowed easily, and we talked about topics ranging from dating to career options. After stopping for a quick supper in a little family café in Giddings, we got back on the road. It was dusk now.

I reached for an omniscient tone: "I've figured out eternity," I said to Peggy. "If you want, I'll be glad to explain it to you."

Peggy said she could hardly wait.

I had spoken prematurely—had never really tried to pull my thoughts together in any organized way—but now seemed like the time to make a half-serious attempt.

I told her about Gary's dream of his father across time, and about the conclusions I had reached. I explained that in dreams and fantasies, time is unbound by linearity and we have no trouble at all letting time slide around. Similarly, in dreams we have an ability to recognize someone's presence, even if he or she looks quite different. Perhaps the unconscious provides hints of what eternity is like.

Peggy and I dabbled with these ideas for awhile. Who knew? Perhaps they were more than just idle speculation. We talked for awhile about her experiences as a nurse with death.

By this time, we were about fifteen miles west of Edna. There were no lights from houses or other cars, and as usual in such night circumstances, I looked out of the car window to see how many stars were visible. There were thousands, more than I had seen in twenty years!

I stopped the car, and Peggy and I got out to look. Thousands and thousands of brilliantly twinkling lights, tossed against the black velvet of the sky. I told Peggy of what someone (Emerson?) said, that if such skies were visible very rarely, the whole planet would stay up all night to marvel. As we stood there looking up, for the first time in months I could breathe deeply. The hum inside my chest that had started in October finally began to fade.

Peggy and I didn't say much, just looked at the stars and soaked up the peace and beauty so we wouldn't ever forget it.

Later, a poem by Octavio Paz rang in my mind:

> *I opened my eyes, I looked up at the sky and saw the night covered with stars.*
> *Live islands, bracelets of flaming islands, stone burning, breathing clusters of live stones.*
> *how many fountains, many brightnesses, comet-tail-hair on a dark back,*
> *how many rivers far up there, and that remoter sounding of water with fire, of light against shade!*
> *Harps, gardens of harps.*

Harps, picking up my mother's melody. Gardens of harps to sing her home.

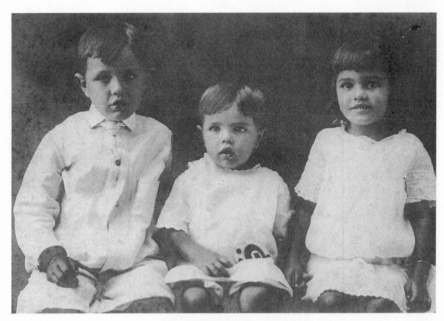

Dixie, at age four, with her two brothers, Ed and Bill.

Dixie, at age nineteen, dressed in Indian Princess costume.

Dixie, at age twenty-seven, her wedding photo.

(below) Dixie, at age thirty-nine, and Lee. Taken in front of the house they had just built.

Dixie, at age forty-seven.

(below) Dixie, at age sixty-seven, and Lee, flanked by Dixie Lee and Donna. This was Dixie and Lee's fortieth anniversary. Dixie is wearing her wedding dress.

Dixie, at age eighty-seven, in her Dallas cottage, with Bubba and Kay.

Dixie Lee, Bubba, and Donna, in 1992.

Anticipatory Grief

❧

To love . . . is to be vulnerable. Love anything, and your heart will certainly be wrung and possibly broken. If you want to make sure of keeping it intact, you must give it to no one . . .

C. S. Lewis

The precursor to grief is always connection. We do not grieve that which we have merely appreciated or admired. The gorgeous sunset fades, the charismatic speaker draws her talk to a close, the flute sonata on the CD gives way to a new piece. The moment passes through us—or we pass through the moment—and we experience the passing with little pain. Contrast such experiences to the outpouring of grief:

O my son Absolom,
My son, my son Absolom!
Would God I had died for thee
Oh Absolom, my son, my son.

The heartbreak in King David's cry when hearing of the death of his estranged son soars far above those sweet twinges we feel in relinquishing small lovely moments.

Grief is the name we give to that pain experienced when we are wrenched away from a closely held connection, especially from one loved over time. Freud used the term "cathexis" to explain human attachments, a term from the Greek word meaning "holding." One becomes "cathected to love objects" when one invests emotional energy in them, when, in effect, one holds them close. Anytime we let someone or something mean something to us, we are cathected, and the loss of that love object may be agonizing. Those people and things that we bond to are what define us as individuals. So grief raises the question: Who are we when they are no longer in our life? How do we then define ourselves?

A new understanding of anticipatory grief

Grief, according to Freud (1917/1957), has a purpose: Mourners must learn to detach their feelings and attachments from the deceased, so that they can become free to reinvest in new relationships. The reality of the loss must be accepted as final and they must "decathect"; pathological grief is that which has reached no closure or resolution. As much as psychoanalysis has evolved since Freud, contemporary psychoanalytic thought is still consistent with this early conceptualization (Baker, 2001) .

My training as a psychologist in the 1970s was not psychoanalytic, but the implications of Freud's theory of mourning were pervasive. Elisabeth Kübler-Ross's (1969) original research on dying patients similarly reinforced Freud's message, at least in my graduate student mind. Acceptance of death was the goal, the final stage of growth; anything less represented an incomplete process. Eventually other writers on grief went on to suggest that Kübler-Ross's stages of death—denial, anger, bargaining, depression, acceptance—generalized to the grief process following any loss. Acceptance was the goal. This seemed to me another way of saying that "decathexis" needed to occur. Acceptance meant one had quit hoping, the pain was over, one had moved on.

Following in a similar "cut the ties" vein was one of Freud's best-known followers, Erik Erikson (1950). His focus was not on grief, but about how individuals move through developmental stages to reach adulthood. He assumed beginning complete dependency on parents, with the infant unable or fearful of distinguishing himself or herself from parents. If all went well, Erikson posited that the child matured to the point where dependency was replaced by "individuation." After outgrowing their dependency on their parents for support and approval—after full "separation/individuation" had transpired—then, and only then, was the appropriate adult development attained.

It is hard to overestimate the impact of this way of thinking. For decades, psychologists and other mental health professionals were taught that dependency was unhealthy, or at least a immature stage of development. Clearly, the healthy thing to do was to attain complete autonomy from all parent figures, including mentors (Levinson, 1978) and possibly religion. "Enmeshment" with the family or other loved ones was seen as symbiotic and destructive and was an indication that an individual had stopped short of the detachment necessary to form an autonomous identity.

An interesting term, used by both Freud and Erikson, was "fixation." Individuals who got stuck or fixated at a certain stage were likely to remain bound by neurotic and conflicting needs until they could somehow be liberated to move on, probably through years of psychoanalysis.

It was a bit of a shock to some of the psychological community when John Bowlby (1969,1980) concluded, based on extensive research, that a large number of *healthy* individuals felt the deceased's presence after death. He stated, "the relationship to the image of the deceased following mourning remains a circumscribed but ongoing experience involving recollection, imaging, and association at conscious and unconscious levels." A number of later researchers have reached the same conclusions.

This was startling and somewhat disturbing to psychologists trained in the earlier model. Healthy people did this? Not just neurotics, fixated at a dependent stage, who were indulging in wishful thinking? What did it mean?

The dilemma for me did not become personal until my mother was dying. With my own patients, it was not important to me to know the "truth" and guide them to it; I saw my role as helping them reach their own understandings of loss in accord with their personal values and beliefs. In my own life, people close to me had died, but I had never tried to conceptualize exactly what that meant to me psychologically.

The context for my ambivalence began early. The summer I turned ten, I was walking through the field between my house and my friend Dorothy's, and I remember praying for something—a new bicycle perhaps—and promising to be good if I could get it. It suddenly occurred to me that I was thinking of God in the same way I had previously thought of Santa Claus. Santa Claus wasn't real. Kids believed in him only because someone told them to and it made them feel good. Maybe the same was true of God? Did people believe, and tell others to believe, only because they needed to in order to feel good? I made a promise to myself on that walk across the field that I would not believe in God until I knew I didn't need Him anymore. This decision, naturally, had implications for what I could allow myself to think might happen after death.

My self-promise led to a rather contradictory duality in me. One part of me became deeply skeptical of what anyone told me I "should" believe. How did I know they were right? People from other religions thought they were right also, so why should I believe one and not the others? Threats of catastrophic consequences in an afterlife if I did not "believe" felt like bullying to me, so not something to be taken very seriously. This part of me, then, thought it was likely that this earthly life was all there was, so I'd better prepare myself to be in relationships that would one day end irrevocably. Later, Freud's and Erikson's understandings of grief fit this way of thinking and made intuitive sense to me. My trying to attain comfort from an attachment with someone who was not around smacked of emotional weakness and a lack of integrity.

The other part of the duality within me continued to identify with many aspects of Christianity and eventually evolved into a deep appreciation of spirituality and mysticism. I relied on my own experience of the sacramental nature of connectedness and the strong feeling I had that there were universal implications to connection. In my personal life and in providing psychotherapy, I came to understand that there was more to reality than can be verified by science or sensory data. Many Christian tenets made good psychological sense; I became an officer in the Presbyterian church.

So I left the question open for myself. When people asked, I sometimes laughingly said I used to considered myself a Presbyterian-Atheist, and now was a Former Presbyterian-Atheist.

I knew my mother's death would require more than my tolerating this kind of ambiguity. What would I get to keep, what would I have to give up? This would be a discovery process, a deeply personal quest. By early 1999, when it became clearer and clearer that Mom would die soon, I kept thinking *I don't know how to do this! What am I supposed to do?*

The question was existential rather than practical. *What stance should I take?* Usually when I was ambivalent, I knew what direction I *wanted* to move in. As a mother of a child, I knew I should tilt myself toward love rather than self-absorption, so that in doubt, I would move in that direction. As a woman going through a divorce, I knew I should tilt myself toward detachment. Now, as daughter of a dying mother, what was the psychologically healthy direction to point myself?

There were, as it turned out, a number of books available; for a partial listing of these, please see the appendix at the end of the book. They seemed to fall into two categories: self-help practical advice, or a more spiritual focus that assumed beliefs I was not sure I shared. The self-help books were often written by individuals who had been catalyzed into writing because of their own losses. Reading these provided the comfort of resonating to others' descriptions of their struggles, but I already knew the survival/coping strategies and had taught them to my patients. Usually, I remembered to do them myself. I was interested in doing more than coping or surviving. *What am I supposed to be <u>doing</u>?*

The image came to me: Anticipatory grief is like being in a small sailboat in a storm at sea. The turbulence and unpredictability would have to be dealt with, since they were not in my control. I could pretend perhaps for short periods of time that I was not in a storm, but reality kept intruding. Practical advice would keep me afloat. If I could accept all my feelings, take care of myself, manage my time commitments, let others help, I would survive. I did not doubt that. But what direction was I supposed to be trying to sail in when I had the choice? I knew I could not just drop anchor and wait out the storm; for better or for worse, that was not my style. Was I supposed to be readying myself for relinquishment? And of what? Surely of Mother's earthly presence and all the things I associated with that. But would I have to give up everything? Was decathexis really the goal?

I thought back to another branch of psychology that I had become immersed in which might offer a different perspective.

At the same time Bowlby's work was calling into question the need for decathexis, several women writers began to question Erikson's developmental theory. They pointed out that his assumption that breaking free from parents as a precursor to growth was a male perspective, a theory written by a man, based on his research with men. (As an aside, Erikson's theory has recently come under similar heavy attack from multicultural psychologists because it seems to represent only a Western concept of maturity and is not generalizable to many Eastern cultures who value community over the individual.)

Chodorow, Gilligan, and the Stone Center were three of the big names in this new movement. Chodorow's (1978) theory on female development lay the groundwork for Gilligan's (1982) research on women's moral development and the Self-in-Relation theory, now called Cultural-Relational theory, of the Stone Center at Wellesley. The Stone Center's (Jordan, et al., 1991; Jordan, 1997; Miller, J.B. & Stiver, I.P., 1997) theory is somewhat similar to psychoanalytic theory in that the bond between mother and child is a prime theoretical focal point, but the writers take issue with a number of traditional assumptions.

To summarize: Chodorow suggests that the female child, in receiving the mother's support and empathy, is able to develop within the uninterrupted context of that relationship. Not that conflict is uncommon, of course, but she can emerge into adulthood by *maintaining* the bond with her primary caregiver and by identifying with her as a woman, rather than by needing to dramatically separate from her in order to claim her own female identity. This ongoing bond with the mother leads to an experience of relatedness and trust that gives the girl a sense of connectedness and security. Counter to Erikson's postulate that autonomy is requisite to adult development, Chodorow suggests that while that may be true for males, for many women the sense of self emerges *within*, not *apart from*, relationships. The girl thus grows up trusting and feeling enhanced by relationships, rather than threatened, and with little sense that her identity as a woman depends on her being separate and autonomous.

The girl's development, according to Chodorow, is in marked contrast to the male child's. He, like his sister, presumably also experiences his mother's love and support. Nonetheless, his time to simply enjoy the luxury of being cared for tends to be short-lived. In order to develop an identity as a male, the theory posits that he will find it necessary to break away from his female caregiver, and to define himself as unquestionably different. There are few insults in most cultures worse than implying that a male is too feminine or too linked to his mother (Hare-Mustin, 1986). Boys feel enormous pressure from peers and adult males—often especially their fathers—to disassociate themselves from "girlish" games and mannerisms and expressiveness and to distance themselves from the support they still clearly need. The dilemma, then, for the male child, is that he comes to feel that in order to ensure his survival as a male, he must be autonomous rather than seek closeness. Unlike his female counterpart, he learns to distrust connectedness and intimacy as dangerous and identity-threatening, and to feel that his survival as a male depends on being able to always function independently.

Gilligan's (1982) research investigating gender differences in moral choices complemented Chodorow's ideas. She found that women tend to base their moral decisions on such criteria as interpersonal connection and relatedness, rather than on the objective principles males more likely rely on. Her findings suggest that women find safety in relationships and that men find psychological safety in independence.

Writers at the Stone Center developed these ideas further, focusing especially on the mother/daughter relationship and on the implications of that relationship for therapy with women. In 1998 I had spent part of a sabbatical semester at the Stone Center to study these ideas further. While they did not address their theory's implications to grief, it seemed obvious that these writers would question whether detachment as a goal of anticipatory grief was necessary or even healthy. I thought about this. What did this mean to me in terms of Mom's death?

It meant that I should honor the connection, and my identity that was so linked to it. I did not have to force myself to end that connection, at least while she was alive. Who I was had emerged within that relationship (among others). To disconnect would be to betray both myself and the connection that had meant so much to me.

Finally. An answer for my existential question about what to *do*.

My analogy for personal growth is that of a tree, adding rings each year. Most of the way we change is not really to alter what was, but to *add* to ourselves. Not all, but a lot of this, is in our control. I would certainly not have chosen to add Mom's death to this year's ring, but I could perhaps choose my stance toward her dying. I wanted 1999, if it was at some point examined in cross-section, to be as healthy as possible.

Looking back now, I can articulate the guidelines I followed, although at the time they were less conscious:

1. Honor the existing connection. Do as much for Mom as I can, as creatively as I can, and do not give up. Continue to try to enhance her quality of living as I always have.

2. Strengthen the connection, if possible, by developing a fuller understanding of who she was, beyond her role as my mom. Could I find ways to understand and appreciate her across her lifespan and in different contexts? Could I wrap my mind around the totality of her? Might I even be able to find *new* ways to connect with her?

3. Actualize the best part of my own identity. Try to find constructive ways to live out the anger, the protectiveness, the love. Passivity was a luxury to be avoided; I wanted to be as proactive as possible so that I felt *more* me, not less.

4. Accept that her ultimate death was out of my control. Much as I wanted to, I could not stop it.

5. Finally, do all the practical things suggested in the self-help books. I knew them already, but I began to realize that I sometimes got too caught up in struggles to remember to do them myself. Particularly, I would have to be patient in the ambiguity of my struggle to connect with her in the face of her diminishing ability or inclination to participate.

For those of you interested in a scholarly discussion of anticipatory grief, Rando (1986, 1988) has an elegant and multifaceted model. It confirms not only my own experience, but that of most of my patients. Anticipatory grief is not a unitary concept, she argues, but defines itself across two perspectives (patient and family), three time foci (past, present, and future), and three classes of influencing variables (psychological, social, and physiological). Very briefly, she contends that "anticipatory" is a misnomer: we are grieving not just the anticipated future death, but also losses that have already occurred in the past and are occurring in the present. With Mom, my grief about the past came from recognizing that the vibrant and healthy woman who enjoyed living in so many ways—painting, writing, traveling, working on genealogy—had already lost the ability to do those things and the desire to do them. Present grief was experienced each weekend I visited, as I was aware of her diminishing presence, of her increasingly restricted enjoyable activities, and finally of her anguish resulting from her incomprehensible inability to die. Grief about the future included thoughts that if my son had children, she would never know them. She would not be there to be proud of me in my accomplishments, she would not be able to answer my questions about family history, I couldn't call her up and ask for a recipe.

Another part of Rando's theory that I resonate to is her description of three sets of processes that take place during anticipatory grief. First are the *individual*, intrapsychic processes, which will be different for each family member. For me, this is what I have just referred to as my existential quest. Secondly, there is the process that takes place in *interacting with the dying family member*. For Rando, as for me, this implies continued involvement, not detachment. Finally, the individual's dying stimulates a series of *family and social processes*. My relationship with my siblings and son and friends changed in the months preceding Mom's death. If someone had wanted to fully understand what I was going through, he or she would have had to grasp the essence of all of this for me. Saying that I was experiencing "anticipatory grief" would not have come close to capturing all the nuances and struggles, unique for me, as it is for everyone.

Kerr (1994) makes the point that knowing ahead of time before someone dies does not necessarily mean that anticipatory grief is taking place: some people keep the implications of an impending death at such a distance that they feel few specific emotions. This is one reason why so many of the research studies about anticipatory grief are contradictory: Researchers confounded time with a psychological process. Because of this, as well as other design flaws, many of the studies on this topic don't offer much enlightenment (Sweeting &

Gilhooly, 1990). What does seem to be a consistent scientific finding is that a loved one's completely unexpected death, with no time at all to prepare, is harder than if one has at least a week to begin to accommodate to the impending loss (Marshall, Cantanzaro, & Lamb, 1997). This is especially true if the person was one's child, and even truer if the death was traumatic and/or viewed as preventable (Davis, 2001). (For those of you interested in a combination memoir/theory regarding sudden parental loss of a child, read psychologist Kenya Kagan's *Gili's Book*, 1998.)

The experience of anticipatory grief

Much as I believe in psychological research, I have found that on a personal level I am often just as helped by reading memoirs. It is one thing to intellectually understand that anger is a typical reaction in grief; it is an entirely different experience to follow the day-to-day cumulative frustrations of a family caregiver trying to deal with nursing home ineptitude. It is easier to feel the nuances and complexities within the context of the story, an appreciation that helps humanize the rather one-dimensional terms that self-help writers have to sometimes resort to using. I have included several suggested memoirs at the end of the book, all involving midlife loss of a parent, which speak eloquently of the writers' struggles, heartbreak, and tentative resolutions.

At this point, I want to address three aspects of anticipatory grief often addressed in the professional and self-help literature, and illustrate them with examples from memoirs and other stories.

Anger. Perhaps Kübler-Ross was right that anger is sometimes a "stage" as one prepares for one's own death (although considerable research questions this stage theory). When one sees a loved one being ignored or in pain, however, anger is much more likely to be part of the entire process. For me, whenever Mom was being treated badly—by fate or nurse's aides or a medication's side-effects—I felt waves of protective outrage. I experienced a small chill when I recently read one daughter's description of this experience. In a *Times* article entitled "Real Simple," Lindsey Crittenden relates what it was like for her to hear from her mother's oncologist that her mom's Stage IV lung cancer, previously metasticized to her liver, lymph nodes, and bones, had now spread to her brain. When she hung up the phone, she turned and shouted in the empty kitchen: *"Don't you dare do this to her!!"* Yes! That's what it felt like! The protest was instinctive, global, and very urgent.

Another very common way that anger emerges is as general irritability (Gilliland & Fleming, 1998). We are exhausted, emotionally and physically, we are trying to keep our heads above water, but our resources are limited. When unexpected stress occurs that we have not been able to predict or brace ourselves for, we may find ourselves lashing out in unbecoming ways. I allude to a few of my personal irritations on p. 112 of this memoir. As many of the self-help books on caregiving suggest (e.g. Ball, 1990;Berman, 2001), such reactions are lessened when we can receive support from others and when we learn to nurture ourselves in ongoing ways.

Finally, the hardest kind of anger to accept and deal with is anger at the dying parent. Not all of us were lucky enough to have loving, psychologically healthy parents. As their death approaches, their poor treatment of us may even escalate, which adds to the injustices we have been feeling all along. Or perhaps their personality has undergone some changes, and the loving parent we had been accustomed to now treats us—not only with ingratitude toward all we are doing for them—but maybe quite shabbily. Just as we would be angry with poor treatment from anyone else in our lives, we are entitled to our feelings of anger now. How to balance that anger with a need to be a good caregiver nonetheless, can be quite a challenge.

Guilt. My brother commented to me several months after Mom's death that the most persistent feeling he had throughout the process was guilt. Consistent with the literature (Brooks, 1999) he believed that his role as a man was to take care of someone he loved who was in trouble, and he consistently felt that he wasn't doing a good enough job—as evidenced by the fact that Mom kept getting worse. Each time he accepted Mom's decision to limit medical care so that she could die, he felt that he was killing her.

My sister and I never felt this quality of guilt, but we did resonate to Reeve Lindbergh's words, in her memoir *No More Words* (2001) about taking care of her very elderly mother, Anne Morrow Lindbergh. She had a little different take on guilt:

"I think we feel guilty about our aging parents, regardless of their circumstances, not because we have *not* done our best for them, but because we *have*. Our efforts only emphasize the truth that we and they must live with every day. Whatever we have done, whatever we continue to do, it is not enough. It won't change the fact that we cannot keep them alive, not forever." (p. 24)

Another aspect of guilt that many of my patients have described occurs when the caregiving responsibilities have gone on and on and the stress from caregiving has become exhausting. "How can I wish she would hurry up and die when I love her so much?" one of my patients wept. "What kind of a son am I?" It helped him a little to realize that he was not really wishing for her death. Given the choice, he would clearly have opted for her recovery. What he was wanting to have end was not her life, but the stress that resulted from the ongoing—and indefinitely persisting—continuation of his mother's situation. Taking care of a dying loved ones is one of those few circumstances in life that we cannot pace ourselves for. Even when physicians or nurses give us a probable timeline, they are often wrong. When someone will die just cannot be accurately predicted, and that means we cannot tell ourselves when the stress will be over and we can rest. Of course we get exhausted and frustrated! Logically at least, we shouldn't feel guilty about this. (All we have to do is convince our heart.)

Still another form of guilt, especially agonizing, that can arise during this period of a parent's decline is when we have to make decisions that are counter to our parent's wishes. Sometimes this means taking away their car keys, moving them, hospitalizing them, and the like. Especially if the relationship has remained mutually respectful until then, preempting their decisions to control their own life feels like a betrayal of the values that have been so integral to the relationship. We are in the position of redefining the rules under which we treat them, unilaterally and often very quickly. It feels terrible. At one point when my father was very ill before his death, doctors had inserted a feeding tube into his stomach. In his restless semi-consciousness, he kept handling the tube; hospital officials, worried he would dislodge it and cause perotonitis, had restrained his hands. During one of my visits, he was alert enough to look at me and plead, calling me by my childhood name, "Donna Sue, please untie my hands. Sometimes I need to scratch my nose." Turning him down still haunts me.

Identity Issues. Most of the major identity issues occur after the parent's death. That is when we usually realize most clearly how our relationship with the deceased had helped define us, and we have to reexamine who we are. (We will address this more fully in the last chapter.) But for the adult child whose parent undergoes personality changes because of Alzheimer's, strokes, or other debilitating disease, the problem may arise much earlier. Their uncharacteristic behavior or speech or appearance, after years of predictable normalcy, is often very disorienting. It's as if we are living through a small earthquake and the ground we have been standing on has tilted 10 degrees. It's hard to stay balanced.

In another of Reeve Lindbergh's (1998) memoirs, she describes such a reaction to her mother's changes in language that is very, very similar to the Stone Center's:

". . . if I am with her for a long period. . .when there is little or no change of expression on her face, I feel bereft of our relationship. I lose my old, deep sense of attachment, and with it some of my bearings in this life. It is at times truly catastrophic to me that I can no longer find myself reflected, as if in a mirror, in my own mother's face."

One of the ways that we deal with this kind of disorientation is to begin the process that will continue after our parent's death: We rely less on the daily "reality" of our dying parent's presence, and more on our internalized image. Madeleine L'Engle (1974), in her memoir about her mother's dying and death describes this process:

"What is the truth of the ninety-year old woman waiting for me at the house, who is changed beyond recognition and yet who is still my mother?...It has taken me many years to learn that reality is far more than meets the human eye, or ear, or mind, and that the greatest minds have never retained more than fragmentary flashes of what is really real. . .

"The Greeks have a word for the realness of things, the essence . . . of my mother: *ousia*. If I am to be constant in loving and honoring my mother I must not lose sight of *ousia*." (p. 49)

Writers in the psychoanalytic tradition describe this phenomenon as "splitting" (St. Clair, 1996). All children, but especially those of abusive parents, are prone to *split*: the Good Mother is the one that is nurturing and strong and loving; the Bad Mother is the one that sets limits and tells us no, and may hurt us. Thus children can say "I love you, Mommy," and thirty minutes later say, "I hate you, I hate you, I wish you were dead!" and mean both statements. They are speaking to two different images and experiences of the same woman.

At a more sophisticated level, this is the process many adult children do when their parents change in ways that are confusing and scary: the current parent is not seen as the *real* mother or father, whom we know would never behave in such ways. We thus can maintain our equilibrium by trying to treat this new imposter well, but all the while holding onto our conviction that how this current individual responds to us does not require making sense of. It does not count. This is not our *real* parent.

Reeve Lindbergh (2001) describes a dream which illustrates the comfort such splitting can provide:

"I dreamed that we were together on a bench at a railway station. All three of us sat there: first me at one end, then right next to me the mother I had known all my life—vivid, eloquent, well dressed—then at the far end, this little silent one, only half visible. She was pale gray and insubstantial, a fog-person.

" 'You just have to take care of her,' my real mother said to me. She was authentic, I knew. Her voice was clear and compelling, her eyes that dark blue I knew so well. . . I was comforted. . .Her voice was so welcome! It was absolutely familiar. She was telling me a truth I could not doubt. She was giving me an instruction. . . this was my real mother's message to me from her real self, about my task as it related to this vestigial, wraithlike Other Mother, by whom we were both confronted and crowded on the railway bench." (pp. 22-23)

(As an interesting aside, many bereaved *parents* (e.g. Kagan, 1998), in expressing their image of the deceased child, speak of a "dual" image—one that captures their child when he or she was alive, and another, more shadowy image, that reflects their understanding of what their child might be like had she or he lived into the present.)

Caregiving

Caregiving is not the same as anticipatory grief, although writers often confuse the processes. Caregiving—the overseeing or providing of a dying person's daily needs—itself falls disproportionately on women, with 77% of primary caregiving by adult children being done by women (Davenport, 1999). Sons do often provide aid with finances, transportation, and the like, but it is usually daughters who provide the hands-on personal care and for longer periods of time than sons. This is especially true for women of color. African-American women take relatives into their homes at twice the rate of White women (Beck & Beck, 1989), and women of Asian and Indian descent may feel especially strong cultural expectations that they become primary caregivers not only of their own, but also of their husbands' parents (Osako & Liu, 1986).

There are many, many excellent books, web sites, support groups, and other resources for caregivers. (Please see a partial list at end of book.) These provide practical advice and information on coping with the usual stressors, on legal and financial issues, and on some of the psychological shifts that often take place among adult children caregivers. From my own experience and that of many of my patients in such circumstances, I would only add that stepping into this role is generally very stressful, but often rewarding in unexpected ways. My father and I connected most fully in his final year, when his vulnerability was undeniable and I finally felt that what I could give to him would make a difference. I am grateful for one particular incident:

I had been by his hospital room in Dallas on my way home from a job interview. Amazingly, he was alert enough to ask me how the interview had gone, and we chatted briefly. When I left, I leaned over and kissed his forehead, something I very rarely did. I straightened and started to wipe off the bright red lipstick I had left, but stopped to kid him, "I'd better wipe this off quick before Mom comes in and wonders what other woman you've been spending time with!" He laughed, and wouldn't let me remove it. Mom said that all that evening, as nurses and aides came in, he made a point of telling them proudly that the lipstick was left by his daughter, not some Other Woman. Moments like this allowed for connections in ways we had never managed before.

Miller (1981) was the first to use the term "sandwich generation," a term that captures the adult child's family role as responsible caregiver to both children and parents. Yes, definitely this is stressful, especially because one is often also trying to juggle a job, a marriage, and some sort of personal life. But at its best, being part of the sandwich generation is like being hugged from front and back simultaneously. There are difficulties, undeniably, but if we are lucky there is also the experience of being embraced in a family context of support and love. As Barnett & Baruch (1985) pointed out, the opportunity to be connected and provide care in multiple ways can sometimes be both enriching and self-affirming.

Living with anticipatory grief

I once wrote a message for a patient experiencing anticipatory grief, which may be worth sharing:

God made us such that our ability to love far exceeds our capacity to intervene in death. There's no way around it: You will not be able to do everything you want to do to help your dying loved one. Give what you can, as creatively as you can, and then forgive yourself for not being able to do more. Your sense of helplessness does not mean you have failed.

This is a time to be kind to yourself. Leave the self-blame for another day. You are facing one of the most difficult experiences life has to offer, and there is no right or easy way to do it. Try to accept all your feelings as legitimate, even the ones that seem to make no logical sense and which violate your values. Make your moral choices about your behavior, but try to give yourself permission to feel what you will. And if these feelings seem contradictory at times, remember Walt Whitman's words: "I contradict myself? Very well, I contradict myself!"

There will be times you feel overwhelmed and want out. Of course—who wouldn't?! Perhaps your goal can be to become more resilient, not to be indomitable. Let others whom you trust know what you are feeling and accept their offers to help. Rules about doing things absolutely autonomously don't apply to these kinds of situations. Giving is a wonderful thing, but this is also a chance for you to learn more about receiving.

Finally, whatever beauty in your life happens to come along, let it in! Each day will bring at least one tiny blessing—a cardinal in your front yard, a laugh, a child's smile, feeling unexpectedly consoled by a piece of music or a passage in a book or a line from a TV show. Don't miss out on Springtime because you didn't look up to take notice. Good things, splashes of life, are still around you!

Post-Bereavement Grief

And so, wherever I go and wherever you go, the ground between us will always be holy ground.

quoted by Henri Nouwen

So what, after all, does death take away, and what do you get to keep? Clearly, when a loved one dies, we have to give up the physical presence, and all that entails, of the deceased. We have known this all along, of course, but the totality of the experience is still a shock when it happens—and it is not comprehended all at once, but is usually realized progressively over time. He or she will not be there for birthdays anymore, or to exchange thoughts and feelings and hugs with, or to check out memories with. We will not see their faces again, or hear their laughter, or prepare a holiday meal with them. The physical reality of the person, which up until now we had always associated with who they *were*, will be gone. Giving up this earthly connection is usually very painful for us; acclimating to the world without the physical presence of the loved one is both the cause and the function of grief.

Each grief experience is unique. I watch a videotape of Mom relating family history and feel increased connection as I note with pleasure the characteristic look on her face when she searched her mind for a date and the little nod she gave when it was successfully retrieved. *Yes!* I think. I'd forgotten those tiny little gestures that made her presence so unique, and it is gratifying to see them again. My brother, watching the tape with me, feels sorrow. She'll never be able to tell family stories again. My son, caught up in the same story, may feel frustration because there are facts he wants to know that she leaves out. Same woman, same tape, all family members who loved her— and very different reactions.

I sit behind a woman in church who has on a red jacket like one I gave Mom, and the same wavy white hair and thin hands. Later I can't remember a thing about the service except this woman and the melancholy she evoked in me. Why, I wonder, is the experience of seeing Mom on tape comforting, but the experience of seeing a woman who reminds me of her so painful?

My best guess is that the second experience felt like Mom was *almost* physically present, and it was her apparent elusiveness which caused pain. Several months after she died, I returned to Bath Abbey in England, where my sister and I had taken her five years before. I longed for Mom more profoundly than I had at any other time or place. It was as if she was *almost* there, as if wisps of her physical presence must surely remain. The associations and memories of this place had been completely set for me within the context of our physically being there together. In my mind, if I was there she surely must be also.

I have come to understand the poignancy of *almost*, as well as to understand that logic has little power to deal with it. I hold in my hands leather gloves that Mom wore in her twenties. I bring them without thinking to my face and feel slightly pleased. No almostness. Why then, does seeing a little girl skipping beside her mother on a sidewalk bring waves of longing that linger all day? I do not know. We humans are such terribly unpredictable creatures! Such moments are not generalizable from one person to another or even to the same person at another point in time. They touch pockets of sadness and longing inside us that we had been unaware of moments before. In one way or another, such experiences are a tribute to what the other person meant to us, and as such honor both the person and our relationship to the deceased.

But—to answer the second half of my question, what we get to keep: According to the newer understanding of grief, we get to keep the relationship! We get to keep the comfort and guidance that the connection has always offered, although we must learn to access it differently. The opportunity may even come to work through old grievances and misunderstandings and to reach a deeper appreciation and bond with the dead person. Our relationship with them is in our bloodstream and threaded through our being; we couldn't get rid of it if we tried! We get to keep the legacy of values and memories. These may well be experienced as sources of strength and solace— not at all as the wispy, shadowy residue that I had feared was all that would remain after Mom died. The connection can be maintained, although in a non-physical form.

Claiming this connection requires no specific spiritual belief or concrete faith in an after-life, although these may help. Human bonds seem to transcend death in ways that may make no logical sense at all to the bereaved, but which are nonetheless experienced as vital and *real* (Klass & Walter, 2001). Amy Tan in *The Hundred Secret Senses* said it well, as she talked about *hope*:

"I now believe truth lies not in logic but in hope, both past and future. I believe hope can surprise you. It can survive the odds against it, all sorts of contradictions, and certainly any skeptic's rationale of relying on proof through fact."

The new grief model

Gratifyingly, recent research on grief corroborates my own reflections. Largely as a result of this research, psychology's stance on grief is changing, and rather quickly (Klass & Walter, 2001).

In the previous chapter, we discussed how Bowlby's findings (that "normal" widowed persons often reported feeling the presence of the deceased) threw into question the "old" model of grief. Until this time, psychology looked at such experiences with great skepticism, usually as an indication of:

1. Hypercathexis—an intensification of the bond prior to breaking it,
2. Introjection—a pathological internalization of the deceased, or
3. Searching—futile attempts to connect with the deceased that would eventually prove unsuccessful and so be extinguished.

Within the last several years, however, a good deal of writing on bereavement has supported the notion of continuing bonds after death. There have been some fascinating research findings!

Several researchers have found, like Bowlby, that some bereaved persons sense the presence of deceased family members (Rees, 1997). The majority of these encounters are experienced as comforting, and although they tend to diminish over time after the death, a number of well-adjusted individuals report feeling the comforting presence of dead family members decades later. Such experiences are usually not initiated by the living, do not match other searching behavior, and sometimes occur long after the bereaved person has quit active grieving—indications that whatever these experiences are, they are not hallucinations or wishful thinking.

There has not been a great deal of research into the extent to which people *talk* to the dead, although in one study (Schuchter & Zisook, 1993) of widows and widowers, more than a third said they talked regularly with their deceased spouse, a proportion that declined very little thirteen months after the death. Some of these conversations are designed to obtain guidance, some are to reminisce about shared experiences, and some are to inform the deceased of continuing family events like the birth of grandchildren (Francis, et al., 1997). Women are more likely than men to have such conversations in the home (Rees, 1997).

Francis and associates found that when men talked to their fathers, they were particularly likely to visit the cemetery to have a chat when things were not going well in their lives. Interestingly, they seem to follow some unspoken rules regarding these father-son conversations: The man must go alone, there must be no one tending graves close by, and usually some activity—such as cleaning the headstone or planting flowers—is undertaken simultaneously. Under these conditions there seems to be an openness in their conversations which they may not have experienced when the parent was alive.

Another study (Marwit & Klass, 1995) looked at the *function* of the bond that was maintained with the deceased. They found that the bond often was used for moral guidance in one of three different ways—calling forth the memory of the deceased as a general role model, requesting specific moral advice for a current dilemma, or simply using the past relationship as a way to clarify their values (for example, learning to appreciate relationships and beauty rather than to focus on material success). On a more subtle note, claiming the deceased as a valued part of one's biography and identity seems to provide solace. This latter instance is especially facilitated by recounting stories of the dead person, with extra benefit felt if the listener knew the deceased.

The coping process.

Stroebe and associates (2001) offer an understanding of grief that suggests that the bereaved oscillate between two processes—loss- oriented and restoration-oriented. Rather than explain their entire theory at this point, let me note the primary implications of their thoughts:

1. Grief involves a balance of focusing on the loss and focusing on restoring one's life so that it can support new goals and meaning. *Both* processes are necessary. Trying to distract oneself from the implications of the loss is as ill-advised as endless ruminations about how the loss has affected one. Theirs is not a linear stage theory: The challenge is to alternate between the two processes appropriately. Further,

this approach argues that the need for cathartic emotional expression may have been exaggerated and may be truer for women than men in order to diminish grief.

2. Focus on the loss of the deceased can involve both positive and negative feelings, often also in alternating form. For example, speaking of one's distress over a loved one's death can shift into a pleasant focus on the admirable qualities of the individual and the telling of stories about him or her.

3. Much of what grief involves is trying to make sense of the situation—trying to find or create some positive meaning. When this is accomplished, the profound negative feelings about the loss tend to diminish.

4. Another part of the ongoing task is to establish an identity of oneself which includes the relationship with the deceased, but is not limited by it. Ideally, this is a proactive process (as opposed to feeling like the victim of fate), and as such can lead to psychological growth.

5. There is no single "correct" way to grieve, nor is there necessarily an end point to all pain. Grief is both dynamic and fluctuating, and it changes over time.

Some researchers have noted that many bereaved persons indicate that one of the outcomes of their grief has been personal growth. Schaeffer & Moos (2001) point out that the ease of attaining positive outcomes from a crisis depends on both the environmental system in place for the person (e.g., finances, support system, living situation) and the individual's personal resources before the crisis (e.g., self-confidence, resilience, coping skills). Additionally, aspects of the crisis itself can contribute to the difficulty of coping, especially the nature and timing of the crisis, the context within which it occurs, and its suddenness and controllability. Regarding mid-life loss of a parent, then, they would probably predict that the less one had to worry about monetary issues, the stronger one's supportive relationships, the greater of both the ease of death and its predictability, and the bereaved's positive sense of self all contribute to making the loss more manageable.

In agreement with the Stroebes, they emphasize that searching for positive meaning is one of the indicators associated with positive outcomes for the bereaved. They also mention that help-seeking, problem solving, expressing feelings, and forming new relationships are helpful elements that lead to the bereaveds' growth.

What might this growth consist of? How can dealing with loss *enhance* us? Schaeffer & Moos summarize some of the findings in the research literature: increased self-esteem, greater maturity, more compassion, greater appreciation of life, changes in goals, better communication skills, and increased altruism. In short, psychological researchers are finding what many theologians and existentialists have been saying all along: "It is only in the face of death that man's self is born." (Saint Augustine)

Coming to terms with the limits on life helps us acknowledge our vulnerability, clarify our values, assess our priorities, and ultimately make more conscious decisions about how we live our lives. As evidenced by many Americans' reaction to the September 11 tragedy, loss can propel us into realizing what is really important and thus into our subsequent reaching out to others.

Loss of a parent

Several of the books listed after this chapter speak to the specific issues that are often involved in the loss of a parent. Especially if this is the second parent to die, there are family context issues that will arise: The family system will surely shift with the longest-lasting bond now ended for all the family members (Levy, 2000). Even in families that have been very close, there is often unexpected conflict, particularly around the division of property (Brooks, 1999). Old childhood feelings of resentment or dependency or hurt, long buried, may surface under the stress of the family changes. In my experience as a therapist, this is more common than not. One suggestion I sometimes make to patients is that they give themselves (and their families) time to work things out, knowing that it may take months or years for some issues and feelings to be resolved. The task, if they can manage it, is not to avoid all conflict or demand instant resolution, but rather to commit themselves to "hanging in there."

Most of the writers on mid-life loss of a parent comment on the generation shift that becomes obvious after the second parent dies. We are now the older generation, whether we are ready for it or not. With this role often come new responsibilities as we step into the vacuum left by the last parent. More significantly, many mid-life children feel acutely the sense that the "buffer" generation between them and death has vanished; in all probability, we are next. Being part of the sandwich generation may have been stressful, but it lacked the perils of being on the front lines facing death. Mortality issues take on new meaning, as it becomes our own generation whose obituaries begin to appear in newspapers. We may become preoccupied with our own bodies and thinking of how we want (and don't want) to die.

There is one theme that appears in many of these self-help books (e.g.,Bartocci, 2000; Brooks, 1999; Levy, 2000) that I want to take issue with. In contrast to their perspective, the new model of grief and my own experience suggest that we do not have to accept an "orphan role." If in fact the relationship bonds still continue, then we are still daughters and sons, and we still have the potential connection with our deceased parent. After the first wave of missing a parent's physical presence recedes a bit, we may find ways to affirm our roots and legacies that mitigate the sense of being abandoned and alone.

At a personal level, I had begun to deal with this identity issue during the months before Mom died. The poem on page 66 reflects my determination to hold onto my role as her daughter. Part of what I was drawing from when I wrote that was my recent experience in pouring over family trees, as I helped Mom get her things in order and as I accepted the genealogy torch, albeit a little unwillingly. Dixie Correll Davenport would be charted on family trees as my mother forever, for all future generations to know. Hundreds of years from now, people interested in exploring genealogy would see that immutable fact, and may even have a sense of some of the implications of it. Once parenting happens, there's no going back.

Perspectives

The more we have understood or appreciated the essence of a parent (recall L'Engle's use of the Greek term *ousia* in the preceding chapter), the easier the transition may be to experiencing a continuing relationship even when the person is not physically present. What undergirds this process is a version of the "splitting" we alluded to earlier. Instead of identifying our deceased parent entirely within our memories of the parent role, we identify their essence with their *total* life. When we stretch ourselves to understand and appreciate the entire person we are missing—to see him or her beyond the reciprocal roles we had together—our own loss is placed in a different perspective.

The hardest part of the last week of Mom's life was the night we three children sat by her bed watching her struggle to breathe. To get through that experience, I had thrown my mind out of focus. I had dissociated, to use a psychological term. About a week after her death, I was aware that I had not really faced my feelings about that time period; I remember thinking that I would be glad to put that task off for awhile. That night, nonetheless, I dreamed that I was again by Mom's bed, seeing her emaciated body gasping for breath. In my dream, as I began to experience the horror of that moment, someone walked in the room. It was my "real" mother. She stepped between me and the dying mother in the bed and said, "Come with me. You don't need to do this now," and she led me from the room. *Yes!* What a great mom!

Interestingly, about a year later, I again thought, before I went to sleep, that this episode was still unresolved in my heart. I just hadn't been able to make peace with the fact that there was nothing we could have done to help. Again, I dreamed I was by her bed. The whole dream was completely silent, except for the sound of the dying Mom's gasping for air. This time, my "real" mother again entered the scene, but she didn't say anything. Instead, she sat down beside me and held me as a cried. It took a long time to cry out the feelings of despair and love and helplessness and guilt; she sat by me quietly, just rocking me until I was through. The *essence* of my mother came through for me, much as Reeve Lindbergh's did for her.

Sometimes as a therapist I encourage my patients to try to wrap their minds around another's life by writing a brief biography. I encourage speculation, accumulated knowledge, and as much empathy as they can manage. If you are going to love someone, I sometimes say, you should try to love them as they really were, not just through the filter of your subjective needs. See if you can love the whole person, not just the part of the man or woman you knew in your limited role. Try loving them from God's perspective.

In pursuing this challenge with my mother, I was very lucky. I had pictures of her across the years, family letters she had saved, her high school autograph book, correspondence from friends and former students, diaries she had kept in her later years. More fortunately, I had the stories she had told of herself and earlier family members. Luckiest of all for me, she was a woman almost completely free from pettiness and grandiosity, so the stories themselves were not designed to be self-serving. I could pretty much take them at face value. Finally, I had my training as a psychologist to look for patterns that illustrate motivation and values.

So, years ago, I began trying to piece together an emerging picture of the whole Dixie. The last few months of her life that task became a conscious endeavor. I can say with complete certainty that she was a strong, bright, loving woman with an ability to blend self-discipline with creativity and joy. I can list streams of anecdotes to illustrate each trait. But, I remind myself, I must not give in to a desire to idealize her. If I'm going to love her, I want to love her as she really was. I also recognize that her remarkable presence was not entirely her own doing: She was blessed with great genes and a loving family.

The relatively complete picture of Mom means, concretely, that when I am pulled into the unexpected nostalgia of almostness and need to extricate myself, I can choose to focus on an aspect of her outside of our relationship—thus continuing the love but diluting the poignancy of the grief. An example may help. I recently saw a royal blue pantsuit in a style and fabric Mother would have loved. Caught by surprise at the intensity of my feelings, I stood still, momentarily awash in the longing to buy it for her for Mother's Day. Those were very real feelings. To move beyond them so I could teach a class, I pulled up my mental image of Dixie on her front porch at eighteen, hemming the yellow shift Joan mentioned in her introduction and eagerly anticipating leaving for college in a few weeks. Yes, Mom would have loved the blue pantsuit, just as she had enjoyed sewing colorful dresses for herself seventy years before.

This task of wrapping one's mind around the totality of a parent's life, it should be noted, can be especially important if the relationship was more conflicted and the feelings more ambivalent. If we can resist the temptation for simple answers or easy excuses, and instead try to take into account all of the "data," we can begin to sort out what amounts to an hypothesis about the other's life.

To do this, begin with the assumption that major events probably impacted this other person not only in the short term, but also in shaping her or his worldview. Poor parenting and events like traumas and family deaths and serious illnesses are examples of such early life situations that tend to have strong effects. Once one's worldview is in place—with its varied components of rules to live by, behaviors to exhibit (and not exhibit), hopes and dreams to follow and anxieties to avoid—a person's choices begin to make sense. We might not approve of their choices, especially if we have been hurt by them, but it becomes possible to view the other person with perspective and perhaps compassion for their struggles.

"Jean" was a patient I saw some years ago. She was interested in exploring the roots of her fear of conflict and consequent subservience in relationships. As her story emerged, she was one of eight children of very successful, very socially prominent parents. They had little time or inclination to devote to parenting and had made choices that led to Jean's feeling abandoned, invisible, and unworthy. At one point and without explanation, for example, she was sent to live with an aunt for a year. She received no phone calls and only one letter from her parents. Not even a birthday card. Similarly, in a situation involving assault by an uncle, her parents chose to minimize and ignore the situation when she told them.

Jean had come to tolerate and expect being treated badly. Her worldview could be summed up as "Work hard, take care of others so they don't abandon you, and don't expect much back."

As we explored this material in therapy, Jean's anger toward her mother grew. Knowing that I had only her version of events, it still seemed clear to me that her anger was not only justified but overdue. It was not, however, based on a very complete view of her mother as a whole person. Still, with anger as a tool for recognizing bad treatment, she was able to change the way she related to her boyfriend and her mother.

Two years after our work together, Jean contacted me because her mother had died. She felt stuck and unable to accept her death.

Somewhat predictably, she now felt guilty about having allowed herself anger toward her mother. We discussed this for awhile, and then I suggested an approach I often use in therapy. I asked her, without stopping to consciously consider her answer, to finish the sentence, "If I had never gotten angry with Mom. . ." It was startling and freeing to her to hear herself blurt out, "she might still be alive." Jean had stumbled into evidence of the magical thinking most of us still carry around deep inside from childhood—that our anger is so powerful, it might destroy others. Small wonder that she had been feeling guilty!

Later, when she was more at peace, I voiced what I had thought many times, "Are you ever curious how you would feel about your mother if you met her for the first time as a contemporary? If she hadn't been your mother, do you wonder what you'd see?" Jean was intrigued by the challenge. As she pulled together what she knew of her mom's early life, she concluded that her very bright, energetic mother, born into a family that demanded that women defer and subordinate themselves to men, might have felt from an early age that she would have to fight to maintain her identity. She grew up defying the family rules, leaving early for college and marrying late. She learned a lot along the way about assertiveness, achievement, and self-reliance, which served her very well professionally. On the other hand, she knew very little about trust and the ongoing sensitivity and give-and-take required in close relationships. Further, having received little nurturing, at least in a form she could accept, she had little understanding of what it might feel like to be the "giver." Jean and I speculated that a maternal role might have smacked suspiciously to her of the subservience and deference she had fought so hard to avoid.

Ultimately, Jean reached a partial understanding, one that fit the data, of who her mother might have been: A gifted fighter for social justice, a woman adept at coping with a male-dominated system— but also a person with few natural inclinations or learned skills that might have made her a better parent. Perhaps her worldview approximated, "Don't trust others. Stand alone and fight to get what you want." Jean found a way to move beyond her daughter-only perspective to a fuller understanding of the total woman who raised her.

In addition to this search for the whole person of our deceased parent, there is a similar perspective which can be surprisingly helpful. Experiencing ourselves as cradled in a nurturing context often provides solace and perspective.

It wasn't until after Mom's death that I clarified how much sustenance I got from her family stories. I'd lived my whole life hearing her tell them, and as she delved more deeply into genealogy after retirement, I picked up by osmosis a fuller understanding. I thought of stories and sometimes told them myself. But it wasn't until her final year that I "caught" her enthusiasm and understood what they meant to her. For her, and now for me, such stories led to a sense of being supported by heritage. We were part of something greater than ourselves, something that transcended death—a family tradition of good will and integrity and commitment.

Joan Anderson (1999), in her memoir *A Year By the Sea*, relates her experience of consciously using her family heritage to gain strength:

"As I ponder my options, I'm inspired by the stories of others in my gene pool—strong women who faced a good deal more than not being able to pay their bills. My grandmother, who left her womanizing husband after an argument and wheeled her two babies in a pram from Brooklyn to Manhattan, to take shelter with an aunt; my mother, who lied about her age in order to get employment and move up the ladder on Wall Street; and an aunt who, when her father made her reject a scholarship to a good university, thinking she would only get into trouble, disregarded his dictum and ran off to Europe, where she was free to do as she pleased.

"Their collective stories rescue me from any remaining vestiges of victimhood." (pp. 127-128)

The context doesn't have to be family-related for it to offer this sustenance. For many people, religious faith provides a deep sense of coherence and meaning. The more authentically they have reached this (as opposed to swallowing whole what someone told them), the more they are likely to be reassured. Others find their self-transcending context in social causes or a creative process or immersing themselves in nature. The essential ingredient for all of these contexts is that whatever it is one identifies with offers a vital continuity that death cannot ultimately conquer.

It is helpful for grieving individuals to find such a context for themselves. And if the person being mourned shared their vision with them, there is even greater comfort from the sense of connection they can feel with the other *within the context*. When we see ourselves and our parent cradled in the same context, we are likely to feel increased connection and comfort. The context still holds, even if death separates the two of us physically.

The song I mentioned on page 28 is an example of this perspective.

To be sure, such sense of connection lacks the immediacy of seeing and hearing and touching the other person. We are earthly creatures, we have known each other in earthly ways, and we may desperately miss those earthly ways of relating, especially at first.

Life-affirming choices

Grief often has a way of reducing us. We feel diminished, less than we were. This can be manifested as depression—or to use the old term for it, melancholy—or withdrawal. We feel less alive, less interested in things outside us as we pull our energies inward to cope with the pain. This is a natural part of the grief process and not necessarily unhealthy. After time, we usually gradually reenter the world, a world that may feel quite different now that our loved one is not in it.

There are three processes I have identified that seem to be innately life-enhancing, life-affirming. They push back the walls that are closing in; they throw their weight on the side of life rather than death.

The first of these is *creativity.* Combs & Friedman (1990) speak to the healing potential of symbols, ceremonies, and rituals. When we do something creative with our pain, we allow things to shift and even be transformed within us. One patient said, in referring to a painting she had completed of one of her father's favorite scenes, "It's like I'm shouting defiantly into the void. Like I'm yelling, 'No, you cannot take him away or dim what we felt. See! I still love him!'"

I encourage patients and participants in a grief group which I lead to find unique, creative ways to honor or memorialize their deceased loved one. One person is collecting all the pithy pieces of advice her father was known for dispensing, and making a notebook of them for her siblings and the grandchildren. Another found solace in providing a party on her mother's birthday for Head Start, an organization her mother had helped bring to their community. Still another took her grandmother's handkerchiefs and made a quilt out of them. I enjoyed, in the months after Mom's death, matting and framing a number of heirlooms, including her grandmother's crocheted work, a hand-painted postcard sent to Aunt Cord in 1905, and Confederate and Republic of Texas currency that had been saved through all the years. The hotel in Bryan where Mom and Dad spent their wedding night was being refurbished in antiques in 2000, and I offered to contribute a wedding present that my parents would have had with them in the car that Christmas night they stayed there in 1937.

Contributions to a deceased's favorite charity or setting up a memorial fund may feel less personal, but still allow for the honoring of the loved one's special personality. Undertaking a task the deceased always wanted to perform is another example. Becoming involved in—or establishing—an organization for a particular purpose, such as MADD, is another example of the productive use of pain. What is important is that the gift or symbol or ritual reflect the personality of both the bereaved and the deceased. Somehow, when that happens, feelings are creatively transformed into a tangible tribute, and the continuing connection is affirmed.

The second of these life-affirming processes is *learning* something new, whether or not it is connected with the parent. A patient I mentioned earlier learned to play the piano. Others have developed new interests in travel, or taken up gardening, or studied a subject matter they had always been intrigued by. When we can find a coal of interest inside us and fan it into flame through new learning, we invite life back inside. The process involves an opening up, a proactive receptivity which is antithetical to depression and withdrawal from life. This is part of the restoration-oriented half of the grief process. It cannot be rushed, but watching ourselves for a readiness inside and then pursuing it is a choice we can make.

Finally and similarly, *loving someone or something new* results in the same kind of vitality. Like learning, we open ourselves back up to allow the possibility of being connected again. When I was seventeen, I asked an older friend going through a divorce how he would learn to un-love. I remember his answer: The task isn't to un-love; you learn to re-love. Such love may or may not resemble the relationship we are grieving. Often, I think, it sneaks in through the back door when we are not looking. We find a new friend, we get adopted by a stray cat, we fall into a relationship where we mentor someone younger. Regardless of the relationship, we allow new connection. Loving in new ways signifies a willingness to move from the self-absorption of our grief back into the risk and give-and-take that all rewarding relationships entail.

Speculations on the unknown

I am not sure what happens when and after we die. I have read the research on near death experiences, and like others, hope that since a number of these anecdotes have common elements, maybe the tunnel-light-life review-reunion aspects will turn out to be true. On the other hand, I have read scientific medical hypotheses that these experiences are merely physical and psychological mechanisms of the brain shutting down. So I keep an open mind.

What I am more sure of is that there is more to reality (Reality?) than we can ascertain with our limited human senses. Some kinds of communication take place, sometimes in therapy, that transcend our usual ways of relating. Connection seems to me to be what feels "right" to people and leads to psychological and spiritual growth. I think that connection, or love, does have something to do with what I call God and that the best human connections somehow directly reflect this greater truth.

At a personal level, I have not missed Mom as much as I thought I would. Part of this is because by the time her death came, I had already given up everything except the agony of watching her body refuse to die. Her death brought little that was new to my awareness that had to be relinquished, it only allowed the agony to stop and the hope for new possibilities to begin. More importantly, however, I have not missed her because I still "have" her; we are still somehow connected. She does not feel absent in my inner life. Blessedly, what I had heard was true, at least for me: Daughters of good mothers are never alone.

There are other ideas I have that I am less sure about. These hunches, or "inklings," as my friend Ken would call them, come from my understanding of ambiguous psychological processes—aspects of the unconscious seen in dreams, under hypnosis, during times of self-actualization.

As I wrote earlier, in dreams we can sense another's presence even if physically the person is unrecognizable. I take this a step farther and speculate that we may not need physical bodies to recognize and feel connected with others if there is some piece of consciousness that continues after death. I think human connections are a little like the imprinting that baby ducks evidence: Once the attachment is there, it takes on its own reality and our internal radars can respond to another's presence in remarkable ways.

Similarly, time takes on new dimensions in dreams and under hypnosis; we can step out of chronological orderings quite easily and let time slide around in ways that would be very upsetting in our usual worlds. Dementia is another state which often leads to people feeling that the present is much less substantial than the past and really not worth attending to. This is, of course, explainable physiologically as the loss of short-term memory, but it also fits with the psychology of time-transcendence.

I used to worry a good deal as a child about "eternity." I didn't want to just cease living, but living forever seemed boring and frightening to me. All I could imagine was everlasting sameness, which I thought would get old fast, even if it was blissful. Now I think that our human understanding of time may be only an earthly artifice to help us manage conscious living in this world; unconsciously, we do fine without linear time. Outside this world, I think it likely that chronological time is meaningless.

There is another human experience which may shed some light on this time issue. In those moments when we are self-actualizing, when we completely give ourselves over to a pleasurable experience, we lose track of time. Later, we look up at the clock and are startled to find that hours may have passed. Psychologists sometimes call this the "flow experience." We flow through time, rather than walk in our usual clumsy, plodding ways. It's as if we have slipped into an understanding of how to truly *be*, how to synchronize ourselves with the universe, in a way the feels harmonious and easy. Interestingly, we do not merge in the sense of losing who we are; we become *more* of who we are.

Some people experience this quasi-mystical state during intense sexual union with a partner they love. They temporarily lose their defensive boundaries in a way that they later describe as floating, flying, effortless dancing, etc. Time and connection move into a different dimension. I think of a French term for orgasm, *la petite morte*— the little death. Perhaps the French had the same kind of inkling I am talking about: Death that is not the end, but rather a stepping out of routine ways of experiencing into something much more enhancing. Rollo May said someplace that sex and death were two aspects of the *mysterium tremendum*.

So what will it be like on the other side of death? If my inklings bear any similarity to the truth, then if we can still *be*, we will feel connected to recognizable others and we will have a sense of being aligned with the universe in a timeless way that allows for continued enhancement and joy and connection.

Each profession offers its own keyhole view into the universe. I am a psychologist, so the "inklings" I have are from that discipline. If there was a way to open the door and peer in, rather than crouch down and squint through the keyhole, I am not sure I would do it. Psychologically, grief provides us with an opportunity to learn what is really important to us, to affirm our deepest relationships, and to grapple with ultimate issues, perhaps finding meaningful answers. It is, I believe, this struggle to maintain connection in the face of death which defines our humanity and has the capacity to offer transcendence.

Suggested Further Reading

Grief—Overview

Coping with Loss—Nolen-Hoeksema, S. & Davis, C.G. (1999) Mahwah, NJ: Erlbaum.

How To Go on Living When Someone You Love Dies—Therese Rando(1991) NY: Doubleday.

I Can't Stop Crying—John Martin & Frank Ferris (1992) CT: Firefly Books.

Making Loss Matter—Rabbi David Wolpe (2000) NJ: Penguin Putnam.

Meaning Reconstruction and the Experience of Loss—Robert Neimeyer, ed. (2001) Washington D.C.: APA Press

Mending the Torn Fabric—Brabant, Sarah (1996) Amityville, NY: Baywood.

No Time for Good-byes—Janice Lord (2000) CA: Pathfinder.

Parting Company—Cynthia Pearson and Margaret Stubbs (1999) WA: Seal Press.

A Path Through Loss—Nancy Reeves(2001) Canada: Northstone.

Roses in December—Marilyn Heavlin (1998) OR: Harvest House.

Understanding Grief—Alan Wolfelt (1992) NY: Taylor & Francis.

Self-Help—Midilife Loss of Parent

African-American Daughters and Elderly Mothers—Sharon Smith(1998) CT: Garland.

Coping When a Parent Dies—Janet Grosshandler-Smith (1995) NY: Rosen.

Fading Away—Betty Davies, Joanne Reimer, Pamela Brown, & Nola Martens (2002) NY: Baywood Publishing

Fatherless Women—Clea Simon (2001) NY: John Wiley & Sons.

Finding Your Way After Your Parent Dies—Richard Gilbert & Darcie Sims (1999) IN: Ave Maria Press.

How to Survive the Loss of a Parent—Lois Akner (1993) NY: William Morrow.

Longing to Live . . .Learning to Die—Donn Weinholtz (2002) NE: iUniverse.

Losing a Parent—Alexandra Kennedy (1991) CA: Harper Collins.

Losing Your Parents, Finding Yourself—Victoria Secunda (2000) NY: Hyperion.

Midlife Orphan—Jane Brooks (1999) NJ: Penguin Putnam.

Midlife Women and the Death of Mother—Martha Robbins (1990) NY: Peter Lang.

A Mother Loss Workbook—Diane Hambrook, Gail Eisenberg, & Herma Rosenthal(1997) NY: Harper Collins.

Nobody's Child Anymore—Barbara Bartocci (2000) IN: Sorin Books.

The Orphaned Adult—Alexander Levy (2000) NY: Perseus.

Recovering from the Loss of a Parent—Katherine Donnelly (2000) NE: iUniverse.

When Parents Die—Edward Myers(1997) NJ: Penguin Putnam.

When Your Parent Dies—Cathleen Curry (1993) IN: Ave Maria Press.

Memoirs—Midlife Loss of Parent

Chronicle of My Mother—Inoue Yasushi (1983) NY: Kodansha America.

Final Rounds—James Dodson (1997) NY: Bantam Books.

Heavy Snow—John Haugse (1999) CT: Health Communications.

In Lieu of Flowers—Nancy Cobb (2000) NY: Pantheon Books.

Into That Good Night—Ron Rozelle (2000) Huntsville, TX: TX Review

Letters to Harry—Janet Graham (1998) VA: Time-Life Books.

No More Words—Reeve Lindbergh (2001) NJ: Simon & Schuster Trade.

Summer of the Great-Grandmother—Madeleine L'Engle (1987) CA: Harper Collins.

You Are So Beautiful Without Your Hair—Suzane Piela (1999) NC: Bluestar Communications Corporation.

Self-help—Caregiving

Blessed Are the Caregivers—Danny Cain & Bob Russell (1995) KY: N B Publishing.

The Caregiver's Companion—Betty Moffatt (1997) NJ: Penguin Putnam.

Caring for An Aging Parent—Avis Ball 1990) NY: Prometheus Books.

Caring for Yourself While Caring for Your Aging Parents—Claire Berman (2001) NY: Henry Holt & Company.

Circles of Care—Ann Cason & Reeve Lindbergh (2001) Shambhala Pub.

Helping Yourself Help Others—Rosalyn Carter & Susan Golant (1997) NY: Random House.

How to Care for Aging Parents—Virginia Morris (1996) NY: Workman.

Nursing Homes: Getting Good Care There—Sara Burger, Virginia Fraser, Barbara Frank, & Sara Hunt(1996) CA: Impact.

Other Relevant Resources

Survival Kit for Caregivers—http://www.aarp.org/mmaturity/sept-oct 00/survivalkit.html

AARP's Legal Searvices Network-1-800-424-3410 (members entitled to free1/2-hour advice

U. S. Dept. of health and Home Services 1-800-677-1116 (medicare info)

http://*www.careofdying.org*

http://*www.caregiver911.com*—online caregiver magazine

http://*www.nfcacares.org/*

http://*www.hospicefoundation.org*

http://*www.nhpco.org*

http://*www.lastacts.org*

http://*www.findingourway.net*

http://*www.aoa.dhhs.gov*

http://*www.rivendell.org*

http:// *www.bereavementmag.com*

http://www.nfda.org/resources/index.html

http://www.grief.org.au/internetl.htm

http://www.extension.iastate.edu/Publications/PM1660D.pdf

http://www.ec-online.net/Connections/bookstore.htm

http://www.aarp.org/griefandloss/

http://www.netkin.com/memorials/homepage.php3

http://www.groww.com/

References

Anderson, J.(1999). *A year by the sea*. NY: Broadway Books.

Baker, J. (2001). Mourning and the transformation of object relationships. *Psychoanalytic Psychology, 18*, 55-73.

Ball, A. (1990). *Caring for an aging parent*. NY: Prometheus.

Barnett, R.C., & Baruch, C.K. (1985). Women's involvement in multiple roles and psychological distress. *Journal of Personal and Social Psychology, 49*, 135-145.

Bartocci, B. (2000). *Nobody's child anymore*. IN: Sorin Books.

Beck, R.W., & Beck, S.J. (1989). The incidence of extended households among middle aged black and white women. *Journal of Family Issues*, 10, 147-168.

Berman, C. (2001). *Caring for yourself while caring for your aging parents*. NY: Henry Holt.

Bowlby, J (1969). *Loss*. NY: Basic Books.

Bowlby, J. (1980). *Attachment*. NY: Basic Books.

Brooks, J. (1999). *Midlife orphan*. NJ: Penguin.

Chodorow, N. (1978). *The reproduction of mothering*. Berkley: U. of Cal.

Combs, G. & Friedman, J. (1999). *Symbol, story, & ceremony*. NY: Norton.

Davenport, D.S. (1999). Dynamics and treatment of middle-generation women. In M. Duffy, Ed. *Handbook of counseling and psychotherapy with older adults*. NY: John Wiley.

Erikson, E. (1950). *Childhood and society*. Gloucester, MA: Peter Smith.

Francis, D., Kellaher, L. & Lee, C. (1997). Talking to people in cemeteries *Journal of the Institute of Burial and Cremation Administration, 65*, 14-25.

Freud, S. (1917/1957). Mourning and melancholia. In J. Strachey (Ed.), *The standard edition of the complete works of Sigmund Freud, 14*. London: Hogarth.

Gilligan, C. (1982). *In a different voice*. Cambridge, MA: Harvard University.

Gilliland, G. & Fleming, S. (1998). A comparison of spousal anticipatory grief and conventional grief. *Death Studies, 6*, 541-569.

Hare-Mustin, R. (1986). The problem of gender in family therapy theory. *Family Process, 26*, 15-27.

Jordan, J. (Ed.). (1997). *Women's growth in diversity*. NY: Guilford.

Kagan, K. (1998). *Gili's book*. NY: Teacher's College, Columbia.

Kerr, R.B. (1994). Meanings daughters attach to a parent's death. *Western Journal of Nursing Research, 4*, 347-360.

Klass, D. & Walter, T. (2001). Process of grieving: How bonds are continued. In Stroebe, M.S., Hansson, R.O., Stroebe, W., & Schut, H. (Eds.), *Handbook of bereavement research*. Washington D.C.: American Psychological Association.

Kübler-Ross, E. (1969). *On death and dying*. NY: MacMillan.

L'Engle, M. (1974). *The summer of the great-grandmother*. San Francisco: Harper & Row.

Levinson, (1978). *The seasons of a man's life*. NY: Alfred Knopf.

Levy, A. (2001). *The orphaned adult*. NY: Perseus.

Lindbergh, R. (1998). *Under a wing*. NJ: Simon & Schuster.

Lindbergh, R. (2001). *No more words*. NJ: Simon & Schuster.

Marshall, M., Cantanzaro, J.J., & Lamb, D. (1997). Anticipatory grief and postdeath adjustment. *Journal of Personal and Interpersonal Loss, 2*, 323-344.

Marwit, S.J. & Klass, D. (1995). Grief and the role of the inner representation of the deceased. *Omega, 30*, 283-298.

Miller, D. (1981). The sandwich generation, *Social Work, 26*, 419-423.

Miller, J.B. (1976). *Toward a new psychology of women*. Boston: Beacon.

Miller, J.B. & Stiver, I. (1997). *The healing connection*. Boston: Beacon.

Osaku, M.M. & Liu, W.T. (1986). Intergenerational relations and the aged among Japanese-Americans. *Research on Aging, 8*, 128-155.

Rando, T. (1988). Anticipatory grief. *Journal of Palliative Care, 4*, 70-73.

Rando, T. (1993). *Treatment of complicated mourning*. Champaign, IL: Research Press.

Rees, W.D. (1997). *Death and bereavement*. London: Whurr.

Schaeffer, J.A. & Moos, R.H. (2001). Bereavement experiences and personal growth. In Stroebe, et al. (Eds.), *Handbook of bereavement research*.

Washington, D.C.: American Psychological Association.

Schucter, S.R. & Zisook, S. (1993). The course of normal grief. In Stroebe, et al. (Eds.), *Handbook of bereavement research.* Washington, D.C.: American Psychological Association.

Sprang, G. & McNeil, J.S. (1995). *The many faces of bereavement.* NY: Brunner/Mazel.

St. Clair, M. (1998). *Object relations and self psychology.* Pacific Grove: Brooks/Cole.

Stroebe, M.S. & Schut, H. (2001). Models of coping with bereavement: A review. In Stroebe, et al. (Eds.), *Handbook of bereavement research.* Washington, D.C.: American Psychological Association.

Sweeting, H.N. & Gilhooly, M.L. (1990). Anticipatory grief: A review. *Social Science and Medicine, 10,* 1073-1080.